Pressure Cooker Cookbook

Pressure Cooker Cookbook

OVER 100 FAST & EASY STOVE-TOP AND ELECTRIC PRESSURE COOKER RECIPES

MENDOCINO
PRESS

Contents

Introduction

You might remember the old-style pressure cookers fitted with a jiggly valve to release pressure during operation. Not only were they noisy, but someone could inadvertently open the cooker with the contents under pressure—steam and foods would erupt, leaving the unhappy cook with more mess than meal.

Yet in the hands of a skilled cook, even those first-generation pressure cookers could yield remarkable results. Thankfully, pressure cookers have become sleek and beautiful, with modern options for both stove-top and electric models. And manufacturers have designed safety valves to prevent users from opening the pot until the pressure has dropped, thereby eliminating the dreaded "ceiling meal." Today's pressure cookers are a cinch to use and offer true convenience for making delicious foods with slow-cooked flavor—but without the lengthy cooking time.

In fact, cooks have been using quick-cooking techniques for more than three hundred years. In 1679 French physicist Denis Papin discovered that food cooked with a small amount of liquid under pressure created hot steam that could speed up the entire process of cooking. Ugly but effective, Papin's "fast cooking" machine was dubbed the "steam digester." Modern pressure cookers still cook large amounts of food in record time, but they are much better looking and easier to use.

The true marvel of the pressure cooker is that it beautifully simulates the flavorful results of traditional slow-cooking techniques, such as simmering and braising. In a pressure cooker, a medium-sized beef roast cooks in 40 minutes, a whole chicken in just 20 minutes, and a stew in just 15 minutes. Overall, a pressure cooker can trim as much as 70 percent off the time it would otherwise take to cook many of these same foods. It's also handy to use a pressure cooker to cook foods you intend to use in certain dishes. For example, you can cook a chicken in the pressure cooker while you chop vegetables for chicken salad or make a creamy white sauce on the stove top. The cooked poultry will be on hand when you are ready to finish assembling the dish.

Compact microwave ovens are useful for thawing frozen foods and reheating leftovers, but if used for cooking, they can deliver bland, rubbery results. Reserve microwaves for the small jobs and let your pressure cooker do the heavy-duty work, such as cooking savory Yankee Pot Roast, pleasingly warm Lentil Salad, Two-Minute Corn on the Cob, or Pork Roast with Apples—and, to conclude any meal on a satisfyingly sweet note, Chocolate Pudding with Whipped Cream. In the *Pressure Cooker Cookbook*, you'll find all of these recipes and more, along with basic and advanced techniques for using your pressure cooker; a pressure cooker timing chart for common foods; and specific guidelines for pressure cooking rice, grains, and beans.

Once you've mastered a few simple techniques for using a pressure cooker, you'll be on your way to cooking many of your favorite foods, including traditionally lengthy and complex dishes, in far less time and with great-tasting results. Welcome to the delights of slow food made easy—and fast.

CHAPTER ONE

Pressure Cooking Made Easy

With conveniences such as push-button controls, programmability, digital displays, and precision thermostats, top-of-the-line electric pressure cookers do many tasks for the cook, and require almost no monitoring to build, maintain, and release pressure. Many have settings for browning, simmering, warming, and sautéing and often come equipped with a dishwasher-safe cooking pot and trivet. Or you can choose a less expensive stove-top model, requiring more hands-on cooking but also slightly less time to achieve pressure.

Modern stove-top pressure cookers adhere to the unofficial 15 psi (pounds per square inch) standard for American models (or about 13 psi for European models), a carryover from early pressure cookers that had just one setting. At a pressure of 15 psi, water in a pressure cooker can reach a temperature of up to 250°F (121°C), depending on altitude.

Electric pressure cookers can vary among manufacturers and models, with some below the 15 psi standard, simply meaning that the cooker will need a little more time to achieve the same results as its stove-top counterpart. Nonetheless, both stove-top and electric pressure cookers save time and energy and help preserve vitamins in foods, so whichever style you choose, you can be sure of cooking satisfying meals with relative ease and in short time.

HOW TO USE YOUR PRESSURE COOKER

Begin by carefully reading the instructions that come with your pressure cooker to learn about the mechanisms and safe use of your particular brand and model. Make sure you understand the working parts and how to use and properly clean them. You may want to practice using your cooker by adding a cup of water to the pot, developing pressure, releasing the pressure, and then safely removing the lid. Once you are acquainted with your particular machine, you are ready to start cooking.

Every pressure cooker recipe in this book indicates the amount of liquid to use, the pressure cooking time (once pressure has been achieved), and the pressure release method. No matter what you're cooking, you'll follow these five basic steps:

1. *Add the liquid before the food.* Unless the recipe says otherwise, put the liquid in the cooking pot first, being sure to use the exact amount called for in the recipe (or the minimum amount required per your instruction manual), then add the food.

2. *Make sure the vent is unobstructed.* Hold the cover of the pressure cooker up to the light and make sure there is nothing blocking the vent pipe. Then position the lid and close it tightly.

3. *Know when to start timing the cooking.* Put the regulator on the vent pipe and heat the pot according to the manufacturer's instructions. As the regulator begins to rock slowly, adjust the heat to maintain a steady rocking movement. Begin timing the cooking once the cooker has achieved a good, steady rocking; think of it as your "rocking rhythm."

4. *Use the recommended release method.* After cooking for the length of time indicated in the recipe, follow the recipe instructions for what method to use for releasing the pressure of the pot to achieve the best results:

- **Natural Release:** Here, the pressure is lowered naturally by simply removing the pot from the heat. It will take 10 to 15 minutes for most pressure cookers to cool to the point where you can unseal the lid. Most recipes in this book call for this release technique.

- **Quick Release:** This technique requires you to manually release pressure so that it drops and you can open the lid. Modern pressure cookers come equipped with a knob or button on top that allows you to release the pressure quickly. (If you have an older stove-top pressure cooker that does not have a manual release mechanism, you can release the pressure quickly by running cold tap water over the pot. If you do this, be sure not to allow any cold water to run into the vent or you may damage your pressure cooker.) When the pressure is normal, unlock and remove the lid.

5. *Follow the manufacturer's instructions for cleaning your pressure cooker.* Some pressure cookers have parts that can be cleaned in the dishwasher; others require hand washing.

BASIC AND ADVANCED TECHNIQUES

Once you master the fundamentals of using a pressure cooker, it's easy and fun to expand your repertoire. Here is an overview of proven techniques and their execution in the pressure cooker.

- **Boiling:** To boil ingredients, fill the pressure cooker two-thirds of the way—and no more—with ingredients. The cooker needs air space to build up pressure. Add water halfway up the ingredients and lightly salt. Cover and seal the cooker and raise the heat to achieve the correct pressure. Cook according to the recipe's timing instructions.

- **Braising:** This technique is ideal for cooking tough meats, as the combined heat and pressure break down the connective tissue in the meat, resulting in tender, delicious morsels. As a bonus, you'll save money by purchasing tougher, less costly cuts of meat that the cooker turns to fork-tender in minutes. First, brown the meat on all sides in a little oil at the bottom of the pressure cooker (select the browning setting if using an electric model, or use a skillet on the stove top), then add liquid, seal the pot, heat until the correct pressure registers, and cook for the time indicated in the recipe.

- **Poaching:** Perfect for delicate foods such as eggs, fish, or baby vegetables, poaching is similar to braising but with the difference that no fats are added to the pot. Poaching liquids can be full-flavored broth, stock, or bouillon.

- **Steaming:** Steaming ensures that vegetables retain their vibrant color and crunch, as well as the highest amounts of nutrients. Steaming in a pressure cooker relies on steam racks (or tiers) placed inside the cooker to keep foods from dropping into the water and boiling. For the best results, use the least amount of water the instructions recommend. Steaming is all about timing: After cooking for the prescribed time, immediately take the food off the heat and use the Quick Release method to stop the food from continuing to cook. Tiered cooking also gives you the option to cook several different foods at once. Depending on the size of your pressure cooker, it's possible to steam two or even three layers of food at once.

- **Steam Roasting:** Use this method on meats rather than vegetables. First, brown the meat on all sides in some oil at the bottom of the pressure cooker (select the browning setting if using an electric model, or use a skillet on the stove top). Position the meat on a rack above the minimum required amount of water in the bottom of the cooker. As the heat rises and hits the meat from all directions, the fat melts and drops into the water, making this is an extremely healthy way to prepare meats.

- **Stewing:** Stewing is the definition of what goes on in a pressure cooker! It is literally the cooking of meats and vegetables in liquid. When you make a stew, however, depending on the ingredients used, you may need to stew foods at different times, thus requiring you to release the lid once or twice during cooking. The Beef Stew recipe on page 20 allows you to cook all the ingredients at one time, so it's a good one to begin with if you're new to pressure cooking.

PRESSURE COOKING RICE, GRAINS, AND BEANS

A pressure cooker can be extremely handy in helping you prepare dishes to be ready to serve at the same time. How many times has your curry been ready and the rice still has 20 minutes to go? How do you make sure your mashed potatoes will be ready to serve with a roast that needs to rest 10 minutes before it's sliced and served? The microwave is too small and a rice cooker too slow. The best option? Your pressure cooker, of course. Once you learn how to quickly prepare side dishes of rice, grains, and beans in your pressure cooker, you will wonder why you haven't been preparing meals this way all along.

Rice

When cooking rice in the pressure cooker, be sure to follow the liquid quantities and cooking times listed below. With a pressure cooker, you can prepare white rice in less than 5 minutes, or take a little longer to make healthier brown rice. Either way, you'll be happy.

To keep the rice from blocking your pressure vent, use a metal bowl that fits in the bottom of the pressure cooker but does not come more than two-thirds of the way up the sides of the cooker. Put the rice in the bowl and pour the liquid (use stock or broth for added flavor) around the bowl in the bottom of the pot. Do *not* cover the bowl inside the cooker as this will stop the flow of hot air and slow down cooking. Cover the cooker and seal; begin timing when you reach 15 psi (see page 3). The liquid, once heated and pressurized, will permeate the rice and cook it. At the end of the cooking time, let the pressure cooker cool and release the lid using the Natural Release method (see page 4).

Rice (1 cup)	Liquid	Timing	Release
Long-grain white (basmati or jasmine)	1½ cups	4 minutes	Natural
Medium-grain white	1½ cups	7 minutes	Natural
Short-grain white	1½ cups	8 minutes	Natural
Medium-grain brown	2 cups	15 minutes	Natural
Short-grain brown	2 cups	18 minutes	Natural

Grains

As with rice, use a metal bowl that fits inside the pressure cooker but does not come more than two-thirds of the way up the sides of the cooker; this will keep the grains from blocking your steam vent. Put the grains in the bowl, but do not cover the bowl. Pour the liquid (use stock or broth for added flavor) around the bowl in the bottom of the pot. Cover the cooker and seal; begin timing when you reach 15 psi (see page 3). At the end of the cooking time, let the pressure cooker cool and release the lid using the Natural Release method (see page 4).

Grain (1 cup)	Liquid	Timing	Release
Amaranth	1¾ cups	4 minutes	Natural
Barley, hulled	2½ cups	25–28 minutes	Natural
Barley, pearl	2 cups	9–12 minutes	Natural
Buckwheat	2 cups	3–4 minutes	Natural
Bulgur	1½ cups	2 minutes	Natural
Millet	2 cups	9–10 minutes	Natural
Oats, whole	1½ cups	20–25 minutes	Natural
Oats, steel-cut	2 cups	4–5 minutes	Natural
Quinoa	1½ cups	1 minute	Natural
Rye berries	1½ cups	20–25 minutes	Natural
Spelt	2 cups	25–30 minutes	Natural
Wheat berries	2 cups	25–30 minutes	Natural

Beans

Dried beans can be purchased for about one-quarter of the cost of canned beans; they are delicious and healthy, and you can avoid taxing the environment with metal cans. Freeze extra cooked beans to use later in salads, soups, and casseroles. Before cooking, soak the beans using whichever method you prefer: Cover the beans with water and boil for 3 minutes and then let sit for 1 hour, or cover the beans with water and let sit overnight. Drain the beans from their soaking liquid. Put the beans and cooking liquid (use stock or broth for added flavor) in the pressure cooker, cover the cooker, and seal; begin timing when you reach 15 psi (see page 3). If you want to make mashed or refried beans, simply double the cooking time. At the end of the cooking time, use the release method indicated for each type in the chart below (see page 4).

Beans (1 pound)	Liquid	Timing	Release
Chickpeas	10 cups	5–7 minutes	Quick
Black, great northern, or kidney	10 cups	8 minutes	Natural
Pinto or adzuki	10 cups	6 minutes	Natural
Black-eyed peas	10 cups	4 minutes	Natural

TIMING CHARTS FOR COMMON FOODS

A healthy diet includes an abundance of vegetables and whole grains, and cooking these foods in your pressure cooker preserves their nutrients while saving you time. Use smaller amounts of meat or use it as a flavoring for beans, rice, and grains. Or cook a large roast in your cooker and have plenty left over for sandwiches throughout the week. Many of the foods listed here are featured in the recipe chapters, which are organized by food type to help you plan weekly menus or use what you have on hand. Here's your go-to list on the timings of foods you'll want to cook in your pressure cooker again and again.

Vegetables

When cooking vegetables in a pressure cooker, a helpful guideline is to use approximately ½ cup of liquid if the vegetable's cooking time is less than 5 minutes; 1 cup of liquid if the cooking time is between 5 and 10 minutes; and 2 cups of liquid for cooking times between 10 and 20 minutes. Check your instruction manual to determine if the model you have requires more liquid. If using frozen vegetables, add a minute or two to the cooking time indicated for fresh vegetables. Remember never to fill the pressure cooker more than two-thirds full, in order to leave sufficient air space for pressure to build. All temperatures are high or 15 psi (see page 3). All releases are Natural (see page 4), unless otherwise specified.

Note: If using an electric pressure cooker, always use Quick Release.

Vegetable	Liquid	Timing	Release
Artichokes, whole	1 cup	8–10 minutes	Natural
Asparagus, whole	½ cup	1–2 minutes	Quick
Beets, ¼-inch slices	½ cup	3–4 minutes	Natural
Beet greens	½ cup	1 minute	Quick
Broccoli, florets or spears	½ cup	2–3 minutes	Natural
Broccoli stalks	1 cup	5–6 minutes	Natural
Brussels sprouts, whole	½ cup	3–4 minutes	Natural
Cabbage, red or green, quartered	½ cup	3–4 minutes	Natural
Carrots, ½-inch slices	½ cup	1–2 minutes	Natural
Cauliflower, florets	½ cup	2–3 minutes	Natural
Celery, 1-inch pieces	½ cup	3 minutes	Natural
Corn kernels	½ cup	1 minute	Natural
Corn on the cob	½ cup	3–4 minutes	Natural
Eggplant, ¼- or ½-inch slices	½ cup	1–2 minutes	Natural
Escarole, chopped	½ cup	1–2 minutes	Quick
Green beans, fresh or frozen	½ cup	2–3 minutes	Quick
Kale, chopped	½ cup	2 minutes	Quick
Leeks, white parts	½ cup	2–4 minutes	Natural
Mixed vegetables, frozen	½ cup	2–3 minutes	Natural
Okra, small pods	½ cup	2–3 minutes	Natural
Onions, medium whole	½ cup	2–3 minutes	Natural
Parsnips, ¼-inch slices	½ cup	2–4 minutes	Natural
Peas, in the pod	½ cup	1 minute	Quick
Peas, green	½ cup	1 minute	Quick
Potatoes, pieces or slices	1 cup	4–7 minutes	Natural
Potatoes, whole	2 cups	10–12 minutes	Natural
Pumpkin, 2-inch slices	½ cup	3–4 minutes	Natural

Vegetable	Liquid	Timing	Release
Rutabaga, 1-inch chunks	1 cup	5 minutes	Natural
Spinach, fresh	½ cup	1 minute	Quick
Spinach, frozen	½ cup	4 minutes	Quick
Squash (acorn), halved	1 cup	7 minutes	Natural
Squash (butternut), 1-inch slices	½ cup	4 minutes	Natural
Sweet potato, 1½-inch slices	1 cup	5 minutes	Natural
Swiss chard	½ cup	2 minutes	Quick
Tomatoes, quartered	½ cup	2 minutes	Natural
Tomatoes, whole	½ cup	3 minutes	Natural
Turnips, quartered	½ cup	3-4 minutes	Natural
Yellow beans (wax), whole or frozen	½ cup	2-3 minutes	Natural
Zucchini, ½-inch slices	½ cup	2 minutes	Natural

Meat and Poultry

For maximum flavor, before pressure cooking meats, brown the meat on all sides in a little oil at the bottom of the pressure cooker or in a pan on the stove top; or select the browning setting if you're using an electric model. It's not necessary to brown poultry before pressure cooking, but you may do so if you like. If you prefer crispier chicken, place it under the broiler for a few minutes after pressure cooking. Begin timing when you reach 15 psi (see page 3).

Meat	Liquid	Timing	Release
Beef, brisket, 2-3 pounds	Cover completely	45-50 minutes	Natural
Beef, brisket, 4-5 pounds	Cover completely	55-70 minutes	Natural
Beef, ground, crumbled or patties	½ cup	6 minutes	Natural
Beef, pot roast, 3-4 pounds	2 cups	35-45 minutes	Natural
Beef, rib roast, 3-4 pounds	2 cups	35-45 minutes	Natural
Beef, short ribs	1¼ cups	20-25 minutes	Natural
Beef, steak, 1-1½-inch slices	1-1½ cups	20 minutes	Natural

Meat	Liquid	Timing	Release
Beef, stew meat, 1½-inch chunks	1 cup	15 minutes	Natural
Ham, uncooked, 3-5 pounds	2½ cups	30-40 minutes	Natural
Ham, fully cooked, 3-5 pounds	2½ cups	35-45 minutes	Natural
Ham, fully cooked, 2-inch slice	½ cup	6 minutes	Natural
Lamb, breast, 2 pounds	2 cups	35 minutes	Natural
Lamb, chops, ½-inch slices	½ cup	5 minutes	Quick
Lamb, leg, 3 pounds	2 cups	20 minutes	Natural
Lamb, steak, ½-inch slice	½ cup	8 minutes	Quick
Lamb, stew meat, 1-inch cubes	1 cup	12-15 minutes	Natural
Lamb, roast, 4-6 pounds	2 cups	45 minutes	Natural
Pork, chops	½ cup	8 minutes	Natural
Pork, loin, 3-4 pounds	1 cup	25-35 minutes	Natural
Pork, bone-in ribs	½ cup	10-12 minutes	Natural
Pork, country-style boneless ribs	1 cup	14 minutes	Natural
Pork, roast, 3-4 pounds	2 cups	30-35 minutes	Natural
Pork, sausage (use rack)	½ cup	8 minutes	Quick
Pork, stew meat, 1½-inch cubes	2 cups	10 minutes	Natural

Poultry	Liquid	Timing	Release
Chicken, boneless cubes/strips	½ cup	3 minutes	Quick
Chicken, bone-in breast	½ cup	6 minutes	Natural
Chicken, boneless breast	½ cup	5 minutes	Natural
Chicken, ground	½ cup	4 minutes	Quick
Chicken, bone-in thighs/drumsticks	½ cup	4 minutes	Quick

Poultry	Liquid	Timing	Release
Chicken, boneless thighs/drumsticks	½ cup	6 minutes	Quick
Chicken, wings	½ cup	4 minutes	Quick
Chicken, whole, 4–5 pounds	Cover completely	30–35 minutes	Natural
Chicken, whole, 3–4 pounds	2 cups	20 minutes	Natural
Duck, pieces (use rack)	½ cup	8 minutes	Natural
Duck, whole (use rack)	1 cup	25 minutes	Natural

Eggs

Pressure steaming fresh eggs is a true treat. Hard-boiled eggs prepared this way will be easy to peel and taste delicious. Use a rack inside the pot for hard-boiling; place eggs in ramekins on the rack when shirring or poaching eggs. Begin timing when you reach 15 psi (see page 3).

Eggs	Liquid	Timing	Release
Hard-boiled (use rack)	Cover completely	5 minutes	Quick
Shirred/poached (use ramekins on rack)	½ cup	2 minutes	Quick

TEN ESSENTIAL PRESSURE COOKER TIPS

A good-quality pressure cooker will last for many years if properly cared for. Using a pressure cooker lets you get in and out of the kitchen fast while serving up wholesome and flavorful meals. Today's pressure cookers are dependable and user friendly and can be used for a variety of cooking tasks, so you don't need a lot of other cookware if you're on a budget or want to save space in the kitchen. Here are ten helpful tips for the use and care of your pressure cooker, which is sure to become a cherished item in your kitchen.

1. *Electric pressure cookers are the easiest to use.* Stove-top models require more monitoring, but some cooks prefer them because they achieve pressure more quickly.

2. *Do not overfill the pressure cooker with food.* Never fill the cooker more than two-thirds full, as space is needed to circulate air and create pressure.

3. *Brown meats and some vegetables, such as carrots and onions, to maximize flavor.* When using a stove-top pressure cooker, brown meats and aromatic vegetables over high heat with a little oil in the bottom of the cooker, and then proceed with your recipe. In an electric pressure cooker, use a separate skillet or the browning setting on the cooker.

4. *Cut food into even-sized pieces.* If you want food to come out of the pressure cooker evenly cooked, cut the pieces the same size. If you want some larger, firmer pieces of food—say, sweet potato—cut both larger and smaller cubes.

5. *Steam foods on a rack.* Pressure cookers are equipped with a rack that fits inside the machine for use in steaming vegetables and eggs. When cooking rice and grains, set a metal bowl, uncovered, on top of the rack to keep the food contained. Metal conducts heat best, but glass or porcelain will also work fine.

6. *Pressure cook before grilling.* A pressure cooker is the perfect way to prep ribs or a large roast for the grill. Slather with rubs and sauces and finish the food on the grill.

7. *Learn stop-and-go cooking.* Practicing this important pressure cooking concept will be invaluable when making some soups or stews, where some ingredients need less cooking time. Become familiar with the best ways to lower temperatures in your cooker so you can add ingredients mid-cooking. Stop-and-go cooking methods vary between electric and stove-top models; your owner's manual will tell you everything you need to succeed.

8. *Know your releases.* To fully master a pressure cooker, you must know when to stop the cooking immediately and when to let the cooker decrease its pressure more slowly by cooling. This is the difference between the Quick Release and Natural Release methods (see page 4).

9. *Add cooking time if you live at a high altitude.* If you are more than 3,000 feet above sea level, you'll need to add a little time to your cooking. A good general rule is to add 5 percent of the overall cooking time for every 1,000 feet above the 2,000-foot mark. For example, if your kitchen is at 3,000 feet and your recipe calls for 30 minutes in the pressure cooker, add 5 percent of the overall time: 30 minutes × 0.05 = 1.5 or $1\frac{1}{2}$ minutes—or a total cooking time of $31\frac{1}{2}$ minutes.

10. *Keep your cooker clean and the top vent free of food.* Be sure to read the manual that comes with the pressure cooker and follow the instructions for cleaning. Never submerge an electric cooker. In addition, it's important to keep the top valve free of food bits so the cooker can build pressure properly.

Always keep in mind that pressure cookers are powerful and potentially dangerous appliances. You should follow all safety instructions that come with your pressure cooker, and exercise caution and common sense at all times.

CHAPTER TWO

Soups, Stews, and Chilies

Ham and Lentil Soup

SERVES 4

PRESSURE TIMING: 26 MINUTES, DIVIDED

This hearty soup requires just a quick stove-top sauté to give the vegetables added flavor. You cook the meat in the pressure cooker, then pull it off the bone and turn it into a satisfying soup chock-full of protein and fiber.

3 POUNDS SMOKED HAM SHANKS

12 CUPS WATER

2 TABLESPOONS OLIVE OIL

1 LARGE ONION, CHOPPED

4 CARROTS, PEELED AND THINLY SLICED

3 CELERY STALKS, THINLY SLICED

3 GARLIC CLOVES, MINCED

2 CUPS DRIED LENTILS

2 TEASPOONS DRIED THYME

ONE 14.5-OUNCE CAN DICED TOMATOES, DRAINED

1 TO 2 TEASPOONS VINEGAR, OR MORE TO TASTE

GROUND BLACK PEPPER TO TASTE

1. Put the ham shanks and water in the pressure cooker, bring the pressure to high (15 psi), and cook for 20 minutes. Use the Quick Release method. Remove the ham from the cooker. Set aside to cool; then pull the meat off the bones. Discard the bones.

2. Measure out 8 cups of the water that the ham shanks were cooked in and set aside; discard the remaining water.

3. In the bottom of the pressure cooker or in a skillet on the stove top, heat the oil over medium heat. Stir in the onion, carrots, celery, and garlic and cook, stirring frequently, for 20 minutes.

4. Combine the onion mixture, ham broth, lentils, and thyme in the pressure cooker; bring the pressure to high (15 psi) and cook for 6 minutes. Use the Natural Release method.

5. Add the tomatoes, cooked ham, vinegar, and black pepper and heat through on the stove top over medium heat (transfer the contents to a stockpot if necessary). Serve immediately.

Potato Cheese Soup

SERVES 4

PRESSURE TIMING: 3 MINUTES

With very little preparation and a short cooking time, this no-fuss soup is an example of maximum yield for minimum effort. Serve it as a first course or as an easy main dish accompanied by a garden salad and toasted bread slices.

4 LARGE POTATOES, PEELED AND CUBED

4 MEDIUM ONIONS, CHOPPED

1 TEASPOON SALT

2 CUPS WATER

5 CUPS MILK

3 CUPS GRATED CHEDDAR CHEESE

2 TABLESPOONS CHOPPED FRESH PARSLEY, FOR GARNISH

1. Combine the potatoes, onions, salt, and water in the pressure cooker; bring the pressure to high (15 psi) and cook for 3 minutes. Use the Natural Release method.

2. Remove the potatoes and onions with a slotted spoon and process in a food processor or blender until smooth. Transfer the potatoes to a medium saucepan, add the milk, and heat over medium-high heat. When the milk is hot but not boiling, stir in the cheese. Continue to stir until the cheese melts. Ladle into bowls and sprinkle the parsley on top to serve.

Beef and Vegetable Soup

SERVES 6-8

PRESSURE TIMING: 15 MINUTES

With beef chuck cooked fork-tender and drowned in flavorful vegetables, this easy soup is mouthwateringly good. For best results, cook the soup at 12 psi instead of the standard 15 psi.

3 TABLESPOONS OLIVE OIL

2 POUNDS BONELESS BEEF CHUCK, CUT INTO ½-INCH CUBES

1 CUP DICED ONION

1 CUP SLICED CARROT

2 CELERY STALKS, DICED

1 LARGE POTATO, CUBED

6 TEASPOONS BEEF BASE

ONE 6-OUNCE CAN TOMATO PASTE

8 CUPS WATER

ONE 14.5-OUNCE CAN DICED TOMATOES, DRAINED

1. In the bottom of the pressure cooker or in a skillet on the stove top, heat the oil over medium-high heat. Add the beef and brown on all sides.

2. Combine the browned meat, onion, carrot, celery, potato, beef base, and tomato paste in the pressure cooker. Add the water, bring the pressure to medium (12 psi), and cook for 15 minutes. Use the Natural Release method.

3. Add the tomatoes to the pot (or transfer all of the contents to a large stock-pot) and heat through on the stove top over medium heat. Serve immediately.

Beef Stew

SERVES 6-8

PRESSURE TIMING: 15 MINUTES

This stew has large, rustic chunks of rump roast and is cooked just a bit longer than soup to achieve its ideal blend of flavors. The bouillon cube will make your cooking liquid more flavorful.

2 TABLESPOONS CANOLA OIL

2 POUNDS BEEF RUMP ROAST, CUT INTO 1-INCH CHUNKS

3 GARLIC CLOVES, MINCED

1 LARGE ONION, DICED

4 CARROTS, PEELED AND CUT INTO 1-INCH PIECES

4 CELERY STALKS, CUT INTO 1-INCH PIECES

4 POTATOES, CUT INTO 1-INCH CHUNKS

2 TEASPOONS DRIED PARSLEY

2 CUPS WATER

1 BEEF BOUILLON CUBE, IF DESIRED

1. In the bottom of a pressure cooker or in a skillet on the stove top, heat the oil over medium-high heat. Add the beef and brown on all sides.

2. Combine the browned meat and the remaining ingredients in the pressure cooker; bring the pressure to high (15 psi) and cook for 15 minutes. Use the Natural Release method. Ladle the stew into bowls and serve.

Chicken Soup

Puréed pumpkin adds a wonderful dimension to this hearty soup and jacks up the nutrition. Remember to dice your foods about the same size so that everything will cook in about the same amount of time.

2 CUPS DICED CARROT

2 CUPS DICED CELERY

1 CUP CHOPPED ONION

1½ CUPS CANNED PUMPKIN PURÉE

3 BONELESS, SKINLESS CHICKEN BREASTS, CUT INTO ½-INCH CUBES

2 CHICKEN BOUILLON CUBES

1 TEASPOON CELERY SEED

1 TEASPOON ONION SALT

FRESH PARSLEY, CHOPPED, AS DESIRED

6 CUPS WATER

12 OUNCES EGG NOODLES

TWO 10.75-OUNCE CANS CREAM OF CHICKEN OR CREAM OF
    MUSHROOM SOUP

1. Combine the carrot, celery, onion, pumpkin, chicken, bouillon, celery seed, onion salt, and parsley in the pressure cooker. Add the water, bring the pressure to high (15 psi), and cook for 21 minutes. Use the Natural Release method.

2. In the meantime, bring a large pot of water to a boil. Add the egg noodles and cook according to the package instructions until al dente. Drain.

3. After releasing the pressure, stir in the noodles and canned soup. Heat through on the stove top over medium heat (transfer the contents of the pressure cooker to a stockpot if necessary) and serve.

Colorado Beef Chili

The hearty simplicity of this chunky chili suggests the wild, wild West. If you'd like to turn up the heat even more, add one seeded, chopped jalapeño pepper. This chili is also delicious served over rice.

2 TABLESPOONS VEGETABLE OIL

2½ POUNDS BEEF CHUCK, CUT INTO 1-INCH CUBES

SALT AND GROUND BLACK PEPPER

1 LARGE ONION, DICED

3 GARLIC CLOVES, DICED

2 TABLESPOONS GROUND ANCHO CHILE PEPPER

1 TABLESPOON PAPRIKA

1 TEASPOON GROUND CUMIN

1 TEASPOON GROUND CHIPOTLE CHILE PEPPER

1 TEASPOON DRIED OREGANO

½ TEASPOON CAYENNE PEPPER

ONE 10-OUNCE CAN DICED TOMATOES WITH GREEN CHILES, DRAINED

1½ CUPS WATER

SOUR CREAM, TORTILLA CHIPS, SHREDDED CHEDDAR CHEESE, AND
    CHOPPED FRESH CILANTRO, FOR SERVING

1. In the bottom of the pressure cooker or in a skillet on the stove top, heat the oil over medium-high heat. When the oil is shiny, add the beef and brown on all sides, seasoning with salt and pepper as it cooks.

2. Combine the browned meat and the remaining ingredients in the pressure cooker; bring the pressure to high (15 psi) and cook for 15 minutes. Use the Natural Release method. Ladle into bowls and serve with accompaniments as desired.

15-Minute New England Clam Chowder

SERVES 6-8

PRESSURE TIMING: 5 MINUTES

This recipe requires just a tiny bit more effort than opening a can of soup, and the results are spectacular. This toothsome chowder shows off what the pressure cooker does best: fast and good. Serve with oyster crackers.

1 CUP DICED BACON OR PANCETTA

1 LARGE ONION, FINELY CHOPPED

SALT AND GROUND BLACK PEPPER

⅓ CUP DRY WHITE WINE

2 LARGE POTATOES, CUBED

THREE 8-OUNCE BOTTLES CLAM JUICE

ONE 10-OUNCE CAN CLAMS, UNDRAINED

½ TEASPOON CAYENNE PEPPER

2 TABLESPOONS UNSALTED BUTTER

2 TABLESPOONS ALL-PURPOSE FLOUR

1 CUP MILK

1 CUP CREAM

1. In the bottom of the pressure cooker or in a skillet on the stove top, fry the bacon over medium-high heat until it releases its fat. Add the onion and season with salt and pepper. Continue cooking until the bacon is crisp and the onion is translucent.

2. Add the wine and simmer, scraping up the browned bits from the sides and bottom of the pan, until the alcohol in the wine cooks off, 3 to 4 minutes.

3. Combine the bacon-onion mixture, potatoes, clam juice, liquid from the canned clams, and cayenne in the pressure cooker. Bring the pressure to high (15 psi) and cook for 5 minutes. Use the Quick Release method.

continued ▶

4. Melt the butter in a small saucepan over medium heat. When it's completely melted, add the flour and stir, cooking, to make a roux.

5. After releasing the pressure, add the clams, the butter-flour roux, the milk, and the cream. Heat on the stove top over medium heat (transfer the contents to a large stockpot if necessary), stirring constantly, until the soup thickens. Serve at once.

Vegetable Soup with Lima Beans and Barley

SERVES 6

PRESSURE TIMING: 13 MINUTES

Brimming with healthful vegetables, this soup can be made from beginning to end—including all the preparation—in just 30 minutes. After tasting, your guests are sure to agree that it was time well spent.

2 TABLESPOONS OLIVE OIL

2 CUPS CHOPPED ONION

3 CELERY STALKS, THINLY SLICED

ONE 14.5-OUNCE CAN DICED TOMATOES, DRAINED

1 CUP DRIED BABY LIMA BEANS

½ CUP PEARL BARLEY

½ BUNCH KALE, STEMS REMOVED AND LEAVES TORN INTO PIECES

2 TEASPOONS DRIED OREGANO

4 CUPS WATER

4 CUPS REDUCED-SODIUM VEGETABLE BROTH

4 LARGE CARROTS, TRIMMED AND SCRUBBED

1 TABLESPOON BALSAMIC VINEGAR

1 CUP GRATED PARMESAN OR ROMANO CHEESE, TO SERVE

1. In the bottom of the pressure cooker or in a skillet on the stove top, heat the oil over medium-high heat. Add the onion and celery and sauté until the onions are soft, 4 to 5 minutes.

2. Combine the onion-celery mixture, tomatoes, lima beans, barley, kale, and oregano in the pressure cooker. Stir in the water and broth and lay the carrots on top of the stew. Bring the pressure to high (15 psi) and cook for 13 minutes. Use the Quick Release method.

3. Remove the carrots and slice into the stew. Stir in the vinegar and ladle into bowls, topping each serving with grated cheese. Offer the remaining cheese alongside.

Lamb Stew

Lamb can be tough, so here is a wonderful way to turn it into a fork-tender stew. After browning the meat, add a few simple ingredients to the pressure cooker, and in 30 minutes, you have a hearty, delicious stew.

2 TABLESPOONS CANOLA OIL

2 POUNDS BONELESS LAMB LEG OR SHOULDER, CUT INTO 1-INCH CHUNKS

1 MEDIUM ACORN SQUASH, PEELED AND CUT INTO 1-INCH CHUNKS

3 LARGE CARROTS, PEELED AND CUT INTO 1-INCH PIECES

2 FRESH ROSEMARY SPRIGS

6 GARLIC CLOVES, THINLY SLICED

¼ CUP WATER

PINCH OF SALT

1. In the bottom of the pressure cooker or in a skillet on the stove top, heat the oil over medium-high heat. Add the meat and brown on all sides.

2. Combine the browned meat and the remaining ingredients in the pressure cooker; bring the pressure to high (15 psi) and cook for 30 minutes. Use the Natural Release method. Remove the rosemary sprigs. Ladle the stew into bowls and serve.

Cauliflower and Swiss Cheese Soup

SERVES 6

PRESSURE TIMING: 12 MINUTES

If you enjoy a creamy soup, this one is for you. After a quick sauté of vegetables, everything goes into the pressure cooker for a mere 12 minutes. Processing the mixture in a blender or food processor will lend the soup creaminess, with melted Swiss cheese as the finishing touch.

2 TABLESPOONS VEGETABLE OIL

1 LARGE ONION, CHOPPED

2 GARLIC CLOVES, MINCED

2 CARROTS, PEELED AND CUT INTO 1-INCH PIECES

2 CELERY STALKS, CUT INTO 1-INCH PIECES

3 CUPS REDUCED-SODIUM CHICKEN BROTH

ONE 10-OUNCE PACKAGE FROZEN CAULIFLOWER

1 TEASPOON DRIED THYME

2 CUPS SHREDDED SWISS CHEESE

SALT AND GROUND BLACK PEPPER

1. In the bottom of the pressure cooker or in a skillet on the stove top, heat the oil over medium-high heat. Add the onion and sauté, stirring frequently, until the onion is soft, about 5 minutes. Add the garlic and cook for 2 minutes more. Add the carrots and celery to the pan and cook for 3 to 4 minutes more.

2. Combine the vegetable mixture, broth, cauliflower, and thyme in the pressure cooker. Bring the pressure to high (15 psi) and cook for 12 minutes. Use the Natural Release method.

continued ▶

3. Once the vegetables are cool enough to handle, transfer to a food processor or blender—in batches if necessary—and process until smooth. Alternatively, you can use a handheld immersion blender to purée the soup right in the pressure cooker.

4. Return the soup to the pressure cooker or a large pot on the stove top and reheat over medium heat. Add the cheese and stir until it melts into the soup. Season with salt and pepper and serve.

CHAPTER THREE

Beans and Legumes

Baked Beans

SERVES 6

PRESSURE TIMING: 30 MINUTES

With a pressure cooker, you can make baked beans even in summer, because the quick cooking time won't overheat your kitchen. With a delicate, distinctive flavor, great northern beans are ideal for this traditional American dish, but you can substitute any white beans with great results.

¼ POUND BACON OR PANCETTA, DICED

1 LARGE ONION, FINELY CHOPPED

1 POUND DRIED GREAT NORTHERN BEANS, SOAKED (PAGE 8)
   AND DRAINED

½ CUP MOLASSES OR ¼ CUP MOLASSES PLUS ¼ CUP BROWN SUGAR

1 TEASPOON BAKING SODA

1 TABLESPOON GRAINY MUSTARD

½ TEASPOON DRY MUSTARD

2 CUPS WATER, OR MORE IF NEEDED

1. In the bottom of the pressure cooker or in a skillet on the stove top, fry the bacon over medium-high heat until it releases its fat. Drain off all but 1 tablespoon of the fat and return the pot to the heat. Add the onion and sauté until soft and translucent, about 5 minutes.

2. Combine the bacon-onion mixture and the remaining ingredients in the pressure cooker. The water should cover the beans by about an inch; add more water if needed. Bring the pressure to high (15 psi) and cook for 30 minutes. Use the Natural Release method. Serve immediately.

Chickpeas and Potatoes (*Aloo Chana*)

SERVES 6

PRESSURE TIMING: 30 MINUTES

Popular in Indian restaurants, this hearty side dish is substantial enough to serve as a vegetarian entrée. Serve with toasted pita wedges.

2 TABLESPOONS VEGETABLE OIL

¼ TEASPOON MUSTARD SEED

½ TO 1 TEASPOON CURRY POWDER

1 TEASPOON GROUND CUMIN

1 LARGE ONION, THINLY SLICED

2 TEASPOONS GARAM MASALA

2 TEASPOONS CHILI POWDER

2 CUPS CHICKPEAS, SOAKED (PAGE 8) AND DRAINED

2 LARGE POTATOES, CUBED

1. In the bottom of the pressure cooker or in a skillet on the stove top, heat the oil over medium-high heat. Add the mustard seed and curry powder to the oil. Cook until the seeds pop, 1 to 2 minutes. Add the cumin and onion. Cook, stirring, until the onion begins to soften, 2 to 3 minutes.

2. Combine the onion mixture, garam masala, and chili powder in the pressure cooker. Stir in the chickpeas and potatoes; bring the pressure to high (15 psi) and cook for 30 minutes. Use the Natural Release method. The potatoes should be slightly mushy. Serve immediately.

Lentil Salad

Warm salads are a welcome accompaniment to wintertime meals, and are also great light fare for any meal throughout the year. The lentils cook in the pressure cooker for just 8 minutes, and the rest of the salad comes together in just another minute or two.

1 POUND DRIED LENTILS

6 CUPS WATER, OR MORE IF NECESSARY

1 CUP SHREDDED CARROT

1 CUP THINLY SLICED CELERY

1 CUP DICED GREEN OR RED BELL PEPPER

¼ CUP EXTRA-VIRGIN OLIVE OIL

2 TABLESPOONS FRESH LEMON JUICE

¼ CUP CHOPPED FRESH PARSLEY

SALT AND GROUND BLACK PEPPER

½ CUP FETA CHEESE

1. Put the lentils in the pressure cooker and add the water. The water should cover the legumes by an inch or so; add more water if necessary. Bring the pressure to high (15 psi) and cook for 8 minutes. Use the Quick Release method.

2. Drain the lentils and transfer to a large bowl. Add the carrot, celery, bell pepper, olive oil, lemon juice, and parsley; season with salt and pepper. Mix gently but thoroughly. Crumble the feta cheese over the top and serve immediately.

Black Bean Burritos

SERVES 6

PRESSURE TIMING: 5 MINUTES

Cook the beans in the pressure cooker, add spices and a sprinkle of cheese, and you have a winning lunch in less than 15 minutes. Offer the fixings alongside and let everyone assemble their own burritos. These beans also make an ideal side dish for grilled spicy skirt steaks.

1 POUND DRIED BLACK BEANS, SOAKED (PAGE 8) AND DRAINED

1 ONION, CUT IN HALF

1 CELERY STALK, CUT IN HALF

2½ CUPS WATER, DIVIDED

2 TABLESPOONS BACON FAT OR EXTRA-VIRGIN OLIVE OIL

SALT AND GROUND BLACK PEPPER

6 TORTILLAS, WARMED

¼ CUP CHOPPED FRESH CILANTRO

¼ CUP CRUMBLED QUESO FRESCO OR SHREDDED MILD
   CHEDDAR CHEESE

1. Combine the beans, onion, celery, and 2 cups of the water in the pressure cooker. Bring the pressure to high (15 psi) and cook for 5 minutes. Use the Natural Release method.

2. In a large skillet, heat the bacon fat or olive oil over medium heat. Drain the beans and transfer them to the skillet. Using a potato masher or the back of a large fork, begin mashing the beans into a coarse purée, adding as much of the remaining ½ cup water as necessary to achieve the desired consistency. Season with salt and pepper.

3. Transfer the beans to a serving bowl. Serve with the warm tortillas, cilantro, and cheese, allowing diners to make their own burritos.

Vegetarian Cowboy Beans

SERVES 6

PRESSURE TIMING: 5 MINUTES

Summoning visions of a cattle drive, this quick-cooking vegetarian version of cowboy beans is tangy and satisfying sans the traditional ground beef. To preserve tenderness, salt the beans after cooking.

1 POUND DRIED PINTO BEANS, SOAKED (PAGE 8) AND DRAINED

1 LARGE ONION, CHOPPED

1 CUP CHOPPED FRESH CILANTRO

1 CUP WATER

1 TEASPOON SALT

1 TEASPOON GROUND CUMIN

1 TABLESPOON EXTRA-VIRGIN OLIVE OIL

¼ CUP CHOPPED FRESH PARSLEY

1 SMALL JALAPEÑO PEPPER, SEEDED AND FINELY DICED (OPTIONAL)

1. Combine the beans, onion, cilantro, and water in the pressure cooker; bring the pressure to high (15 psi) and cook for 5 minutes. Use the Quick Release method.

2. Pour the bean mixture into a large bowl. Add the salt, cumin, and oil and toss. Add the parsley and jalapeño (if using) and toss again. Serve immediately.

Hoppin' John

SERVES 6

PRESSURE TIMING: 26 MINUTES, DIVIDED

This iconic rice-and-beans dish of the American South is traditionally served on New Year's Day in hopes of ringing in a prosperous year. Note that you will cook the black-eyed peas at high pressure (15 psi), then finish the dish by cooking the rice at low pressure (8 psi).

2 TABLESPOONS VEGETABLE OIL, BACON FAT, OR UNSALTED BUTTER

1 LARGE ONION, CHOPPED

3 GARLIC CLOVES, MINCED

1 CUP THINLY SLICED CELERY

1 POUND DRIED BLACK-EYED PEAS, SOAKED (PAGE 8) AND DRAINED

½ POUND BAKED OR BOILED HAM, CUBED

2½ CUPS REDUCED-SODIUM CHICKEN BROTH

1 CUP LONG-GRAIN WHITE RICE

½ TEASPOON SALT

½ TEASPOON CAYENNE PEPPER

¼ CUP CHOPPED FRESH PARSLEY

1. In the bottom of the pressure cooker or in a large skillet on the stove top, heat the oil over medium-high heat. Add the onion, garlic, and celery and cook until softened, about 5 minutes.

2. Combine the vegetables, black-eyed peas, ham, and broth in the pressure cooker. Bring the pressure to high (psi 15) and cook for 10 minutes. Use the Natural Release method.

3. Add the rice, salt, and cayenne. Bring the pressure to low (8 psi) and cook for 16 minutes. Use the Quick Release method. Spoon the rice and beans into bowls and top with parsley. Serve.

Red Beans and Sausage

SERVES 6

PRESSURE TIMING: 30 MINUTES

This recipe is handy because you do not need to soak the beans overnight. Instead, they spend a little more time in the pressure cooker, absorbing all of the wonderful flavors in the other ingredients. Serve this over rice for a quick, rib-sticking meal.

1 POUND DRIED RED KIDNEY BEANS, RINSED AND DRAINED

1 POUND SMOKED SAUSAGE, SLICED

2 CELERY STALKS, CHOPPED

1 GREEN BELL PEPPER, SEEDED AND CHOPPED

1 SMALL ONION, CHOPPED

2 GARLIC CLOVES, MINCED

2 TABLESPOONS CAJUN SEASONING

2 TEASPOONS DRIED PARSLEY

1 TEASPOON SALT

5 CUPS WATER, OR MORE AS NEEDED

Combine all of the ingredients in the pressure cooker; the water should come two-thirds of the way up the sides of the cooker. Bring the pressure to high (15 psi) and cook for 30 minutes. Use the Natural Release method. Serve immediately.

Red Beans and Rice

SERVES 2

PRESSURE TIMING: 40 MINUTES

A backbone of Southern cuisine, this dish is simple to prepare and well worth the extra cooking time it requires. The mixture of beans and rice is protein-packed— and is some of the most economical protein at that. There's no need to soak the beans ahead of time for this recipe.

½ CUP DRIED RED KIDNEY BEANS, RINSED AND DRAINED

4½ CUPS WATER, DIVIDED

1 SMALL (2-BY-2-INCH) PIECE SALT PORK OR BACON

SALT AND GROUND BLACK PEPPER

¼ CUP CHOPPED FRESH PARSLEY

COOKED WHITE RICE, FOR SERVING

1. Combine the beans, 1½ cups of the water, and the salt pork in a metal bowl that fits on the rack in the pressure cooker. Cover the bowl with aluminum foil. Pour the remaining 3 cups water into the bottom of the pressure cooker. Place the bowl on the rack.

2. Bring the pressure to high (15 psi) and cook for 40 minutes. Use the Quick Release method. Season with salt and pepper and stir in the parsley. Serve with the rice.

CHAPTER FOUR

Vegetables

Two-Minute Corn on the Cob

SERVES 6

PRESSURE TIMING: 2 MINUTES

All over Mexico, and in some neighborhoods in Los Angeles, vendors travel the streets selling corn on the cob with butter, lime, salt, and chili powder. You can prepare these to enjoy at home with all the accompaniments or unadorned.

6 EARS CORN, HUSKS AND SILK REMOVED

WATER

1 TEASPOON SALT

1 TABLESPOON UNSALTED BUTTER

1 TEASPOON SUGAR

LIME WEDGES, BUTTER, SALT, GROUND BLACK PEPPER, AND CHILI
    POWDER, FOR SERVING

Put the ears of corn in the pressure cooker and fill halfway with water. Add the salt, butter, and sugar; bring the pressure to high (15 psi) and cook for 2 minutes. Use the Quick Release method. Serve the corn immediately with the desired accompaniments.

Red Potatoes with Butter and Salt

SERVES 6-8

PRESSURE TIMING: 3 MINUTES

This is the simplest, quickest way to cook potatoes. Serve as a side dish slathered with butter and salt, or cool the cooked potatoes to use in a potato salad.

3 POUNDS SMALL RED POTATOES, SCRUBBED

1 CUP WATER

2 TABLESPOONS OLIVE OIL

BUTTER TO TASTE

SALT TO TASTE

Place the potatoes on the rack inside the pressure cooker and add the water and oil. Bring the pressure to high (15 psi) and cook for 3 minutes. Use the Quick Release method. Drain the potatoes and transfer to a bowl. Add butter and salt and toss. Serve immediately.

Brussels Sprouts with Bacon

SERVES 4

PRESSURE TIMING: 4 MINUTES

Bacon and Brussels sprouts were made for each other. Simply fry the bacon, after which this elegant side dish cooks in just 4 minutes.

½ CUP FINELY DICED BACON

1 POUND BRUSSELS SPROUTS, TOUGH OUTER LEAVES REMOVED, HALVED

1 CUP REDUCED-SODIUM CHICKEN OR VEGETABLE BROTH

2 TEASPOONS DIJON MUSTARD

2 TABLESPOONS CHOPPED FRESH DILL

2 TABLESPOONS BUTTER

SALT AND GROUND BLACK PEPPER TO TASTE

1. In the bottom of the pressure cooker or in a skillet on the stove top, cook the bacon over medium-high heat until it starts to brown and crisp. Drain off the bacon fat and reserve for another use.

2. Combine the cooked bacon, Brussels sprouts, broth, and mustard in the pressure cooker; bring the pressure to high (15 psi) and cook for 4 minutes. Use the Quick Release method.

3. Use a slotted spoon to transfer the sprouts and bacon to a serving bowl. Add the dill, butter, salt, and pepper and toss. Serve immediately.

Beets with Dill and Walnuts

SERVES 4-6

PRESSURE TIMING: 10 MINUTES

Working with beets will turn your fingers pink, so use paper towels to rub the skins off. Just roll the beets around in the towel while rubbing the outside with your fingers. These vegetables are well worth the effort because of their sweet flavor and vibrant color; richly hued vegetables contain phytonutrients, which help clean out your cells.

2 POUNDS BEETS (ABOUT 6), SCRUBBED

2½ CUPS WATER

1 TABLESPOON WHITE VINEGAR

1 TABLESPOON FRESH LEMON JUICE

1 TABLESPOON DIJON MUSTARD

SALT AND GROUND BLACK PEPPER

3 TABLESPOONS EXTRA-VIRGIN OLIVE OIL

2 TABLESPOONS CHOPPED FRESH DILL

3 TABLESPOONS CHOPPED WALNUTS

1. Put the beets in the pressure cooker and add the water. Bring the pressure to high (15 psi) and cook for 10 minutes. Use the Quick Release method.

2. When the beets are cool enough to handle, trim the ends and rub off the skins using paper towels. Cut the beets into quarters and put in a serving bowl.

3. In a small bowl, whisk together the vinegar, lemon juice, and mustard. Season with salt and pepper. Slowly drizzle in the olive oil, whisking constantly.

4. Pour the dressing over the beets and toss. Add the dill and walnuts and toss again. Serve.

Spiced Eggplant

Salting and pressing eggplant before cooking will drain out the bitter juices, leaving you with a delicately flavored vegetable dish that works equally well as an entrée or side offering.

2 LARGE EGGPLANTS, PEELED AND CUT INTO 1-INCH CUBES

SALT

2 TABLESPOONS OLIVE OIL

2 GARLIC CLOVES, MINCED

2 ANCHOVIES, DICED

1 TO 3 TABLESPOONS RED PEPPER FLAKES

GROUND BLACK PEPPER

1. Put the eggplant cubes in a colander, generously salt them, and weigh them down with a plate. Leave for at least 30 minutes, or up to 2 hours, to drain out the eggplant's bitter juices. Rinse the eggplant well to remove the excess salt.

2. In the bottom of the pressure cooker or in a large skillet on the stove top, heat the oil over medium-low heat. Add the garlic, anchovies, and red pepper flakes, and sauté for about 2 minutes to flavor the oil, but do not allow it to boil. Increase the heat to medium; add half of the eggplant pieces and sauté until brown and crunchy, 3 to 4 minutes.

3. Combine the browned and unbrowned eggplant cubes in the pressure cooker and season with black pepper. Bring the pressure to high (15 psi) and cook for 3 minutes. Use the Quick Release method. Serve immediately.

Spaghetti Squash with Butter and Parmesan

SERVE 4

PRESSURE TIMING: 8 MINUTES

Sweetly simple, this winter squash is a natural for pressure cooking and doesn't need a lot of additions to taste great. You can buy spaghetti squash year-round; look for a firm, dry rind without cracks or soft spots. Avoid spaghetti squash with a shiny rind, a sign it was picked too soon or has a wax coating. Store in a cool, dry place for up to 3 months.

1 CUP WATER

1 LARGE SPAGHETTI SQUASH (ABOUT 3 POUNDS)

3 TABLESPOONS BUTTER

½ CUP GRATED PARMESAN OR ROMANO CHEESE

¼ CUP CHOPPED FRESH PARSLEY

SALT AND GROUND BLACK PEPPER

1. Pour the water into the bottom of the pressure cooker. Cut the squash in half and scoop out the seeds. Place the squash halves on the rack inside the cooker. Bring the pressure to high (15 psi) and cook for 8 minutes. Use the Quick Release method.

2. Transfer the squash immediately to a large bowl. Add the butter and toss until melted. Add the cheese and parsley and toss again. Season with salt and pepper and serve.

Southern-Style Green Beans and Bacon

SERVES 4–6

PRESSURE TIMING: 5 MINUTES

If you grew up eating Southern food, this is the way you like your green beans. If you've never tried this preparation, you're in for a treat, as the bacon-onion-garlic mix lends a delightful twist to the freshly cooked beans.

4 TO 5 SLICES BACON, DICED
½ CUP DICED ONION
2 GARLIC CLOVES, MINCED
1½ TO 2 POUNDS FRESH GREEN BEANS, TRIMMED
½ CUP WATER
SALT AND GROUND BLACK PEPPER

1. In the bottom of the pressure cooker or in a skillet on the stove top, fry the bacon over medium-high heat. When it releases its fat and begins to crisp, add the onion and garlic and cook for another 2 minutes.

2. Combine the bacon mixture, beans, and water in the pressure cooker; bring the pressure to high (15 psi) and cook for 5 minutes. Use the Quick Release method. Season with salt and pepper and serve.

Sweet Potatoes with Orange Juice and Brown Sugar

SERVES 4

PRESSURE TIMING: 7 MINUTES

Sweet, with a jolt of citrus, these potatoes pair beautifully with pork or poultry.

½ CUP PACKED BROWN SUGAR

½ TEASPOON SALT

½ TEASPOON GROUND CINNAMON

¼ TEASPOON GROUND NUTMEG

1 CUP ORANGE JUICE

2 LARGE SWEET POTATOES, PEELED, QUARTERED, AND CUT INTO
    ½-INCH-THICK SLICES

2 TABLESPOONS BUTTER, CUT INTO SMALL PIECES

1. In a small bowl, combine the brown sugar, salt, cinnamon, and nutmeg. Set aside.

2. Pour the orange juice into the bottom of the pressure cooker. Place the sweet potato slices on the steamer rack in the pressure cooker and sprinkle the sugar mixture over all. Dot the surface of the sweet potato slices with the butter pieces. Bring the pressure to high (15 psi) and cook for 7 minutes. Use the Quick Release method. Use a slotted spoon to transfer the potatoes to a serving bowl.

3. In the bottom of the pressure cooker or in a small saucepan on the stove top, boil the cooking liquid until it becomes thick and syrupy, 5 to 7 minutes. Pour the syrup over the potatoes and serve.

Artichokes with Dipping Sauces

SERVES 4

PRESSURE TIMING: 15 MINUTES

You should be able to fit four medium-sized artichokes on the steamer rack of your pressure cooker. They will be ready to eat in 15 minutes, and you can have either dipping sauce prepared with time to spare.

4 MEDIUM ARTICHOKES

WATER

GARLIC MAYONNAISE DIPPING SAUCE OR LEMON BUTTER
     DIPPING SAUCE (RECIPES FOLLOW)

1. Trim the stems of the artichokes flush with the base. Pull the toughest outer leaves off the artichokes and trim the remaining pointed, sharp leaves. Place the artichokes on the steamer rack in the pressure cooker. Add enough water to come up just below the rack.

2. Bring the pressure to high (15 psi) and cook for 15 minutes. Use the Quick Release method. Serve the artichokes with your choice of dipping sauce.

GARLIC MAYONNAISE DIPPING SAUCE

½ CUP MAYONNAISE

¼ TO ½ TEASPOON CURRY POWDER

GROUND BLACK PEPPER TO TASTE

PINCH OF GARLIC POWDER

SQUIRT OF FRESH LEMON JUICE

In a small bowl, combine all of the ingredients.

LEMON BUTTER DIPPING SAUCE

4 TABLESPOONS UNSALTED BUTTER, MELTED

JUICE OF ½ LEMON

In a small bowl, combine the melted butter and lemon juice.

Sesame Seed Broccoli

SERVES 4

PRESSURE TIMING: 4 MINUTES

Health experts advise eating broccoli a few times a week; vitamin-packed and a natural detoxifier, its cholesterol-lowering ability is a great health enhancer. Here's a fast, delicious way to add this superfood to your table in minutes.

2 TABLESPOONS VEGETABLE OIL

2 GARLIC CLOVES, MINCED

ONE 1-INCH PIECE PEELED FRESH GINGER, GRATED

2 CUPS BROCCOLI FLORETS

6 TABLESPOONS WATER

2 TABLESPOONS REDUCED-SODIUM SOY SAUCE

2 TABLESPOONS SESAME SEEDS

1. In the bottom of the pressure cooker or in a sauté pan on the stove top, heat the oil over medium-high heat until shiny. Add the garlic and ginger and cook for 2 minutes. Add the broccoli florets and sauté just until they turn bright green.

2. Pour the water and soy sauce into the pressure cooker. Put the broccoli florets on the rack inside the cooker. Bring the pressure to high (15 psi) and cook for 4 minutes. Use the Quick Release method.

3. Transfer the broccoli to a serving dish. Top with the sesame seeds and serve immediately.

Kale and Carrots

SERVES 4

PRESSURE TIMING: 8 MINUTES

If you haven't tasted kale before, you may be pleasantly surprised. When cooked in a pressure cooker, the tough stems turn out as tender as the leaves. This quick side dish is nutrient-packed.

2 TABLESPOONS VEGETABLE OIL

1 ONION, THINLY SLICED

4 GARLIC CLOVES, MINCED

2 LARGE CARROTS, PEELED AND CUT INTO ½-INCH PIECES

½ CUP REDUCED-SODIUM CHICKEN BROTH

10 OUNCES KALE, ROUGHLY CHOPPED

SALT AND GROUND BLACK PEPPER

½ TEASPOON RED PEPPER FLAKES

BALSAMIC VINEGAR

1. In the bottom of the pressure cooker or in a skillet on the stove top, heat the oil over medium-high heat. Add the onion and garlic and sauté for 3 minutes. Add the carrots and sauté for 3 more minutes.

2. Pour the chicken broth into the bottom of the pressure cooker. Place the kale on the rack in the pressure cooker. Pour the onion-carrot mixture over the leaves and season with salt and pepper. Bring the pressure to high (15 psi) and cook for 8 minutes. Use the Quick Release method.

3. Transfer the kale and carrots to a serving bowl. Add the red pepper flakes and vinegar to taste; toss and serve.

Collard Greens with Balsamic Vinegar

SERVES 4

PRESSURE TIMING: 20 MINUTES

Collard greens with vinegar are a time-honored dish in the South, and this tasty dish proves why.

1 BUNCH COLLARD GREENS, THICK STEMS REMOVED AND LEAVES TORN
    INTO PIECES
½ TEASPOON SALT
1 TEASPOON SUGAR
1 ONION, THINLY SLICED
4 GARLIC CLOVES, MINCED
½ CUP REDUCED-SODIUM CHICKEN BROTH
2 TABLESPOONS OLIVE OIL
2 TABLESPOONS TOMATO PASTE
2 TABLESPOONS BALSAMIC VINEGAR AND MORE TO SERVE, IF DESIRED

1. In a large bowl, toss the collard greens with the salt and sugar. Let sit for 15 minutes.

2. Combine the greens and the remaining ingredients in the pressure cooker; bring the pressure to high (15 psi) and cook for 20 minutes. Use the Quick Release method.

3. Transfer the greens to a serving bowl and drizzle with more vinegar if desired. Serve immediately.

CHAPTER FIVE

Rice and Risotto

Perfect Rice

SERVES 4

PRESSURE TIMING: 5 MINUTES

Make it your habit to prepare rice in a pressure cooker. It's so simple, and it's ready in 5 minutes. Use any kind of broth or flavored liquid in place of the water in this recipe.

2½ CUPS WATER, DIVIDED
1 CUP RICE
PINCH OF SALT

Pour 1 cup of the water into the bottom of the pressure cooker. Pour the remaining 1½ cups water into a metal bowl; add the rice and salt, and place the bowl on the rack inside the pressure cooker. Bring the pressure to high (15 psi) and cook for 5 minutes. Use the Natural Release method. Fluff the rice with a fork and serve.

Spanish Rice

SERVES 4

PRESSURE TIMING: 5 MINUTES

Spanish-style rice features the addition of tomatoes, onions, and spices. Here, there's also a bit of garlic, which isn't traditional but is very tasty. Use it if you like.

2 TABLESPOONS VEGETABLE OIL

1 ONION, CHOPPED

2 GARLIC CLOVES, MINCED (OPTIONAL)

1 CUP CHOPPED FRESH OR CANNED TOMATOES

2½ CUPS WATER OR BROTH, DIVIDED

2 CUPS MEDIUM- OR LONG-GRAIN WHITE RICE

1½ TEASPOONS SALT

1 TEASPOON DRIED OREGANO

¼ TEASPOON CAYENNE PEPPER

1. In the bottom of the pressure cooker or in a skillet on the stove top, heat the oil over high heat. When the oil shines, add the onion and garlic (if using) and sauté until soft, about 5 minutes. Add the tomatoes and cook, stirring, for 1 minute longer.

2. Combine the onion-tomato mixture with 1 cup of the water in the bottom of the pressure cooker. Pour the remaining 1½ cups water into a metal bowl and add the rice, salt, oregano, and cayenne. Place the bowl on the rack inside the pressure cooker.

3. Bring the pressure to high (15 psi) and cook for 5 minutes. Use the Natural Release method and serve.

Chicken and Rice

SERVES 4

PRESSURE TIMING: 15 MINUTES

You may prefer to cook with brown rice for its nutritional qualities, but if you choose to substitute it in this recipe you will need to pressure cook just a little longer to finish the rice. While you are waiting, applaud yourself for making a healthy choice—although every now and then, white rice is nice.

4 BONE-IN CHICKEN BREASTS

SALT AND GROUND BLACK PEPPER

2 TABLESPOONS VEGETABLE OIL

3 CARROTS, PEELED AND CUT INTO ½-INCH PIECES

1 ONION, CHOPPED

3 GARLIC CLOVES, MINCED

1½ CUPS LONG-GRAIN WHITE RICE

2 CUPS REDUCED-SODIUM CHICKEN BROTH

1 TEASPOON SALT

1 TEASPOON DRIED OREGANO

1 CUP FROZEN PEAS

2 TABLESPOONS MINCED FRESH PARSLEY

2 TABLESPOONS FRESH LIME JUICE

1. Season the chicken with salt and pepper. In the bottom of the pressure cooker or in a skillet on the stove top, heat the oil over medium-high heat. When it shines, add the chicken breasts, skin-side down, and cook until golden brown, about 6 minutes. Remove to a plate and set aside.

2. Drain off all but 1 tablespoon of the fat. Add the carrots, onion, and garlic and sauté until the garlic is fragrant, about 1 minute. Add the rice and stir for 30 seconds, coating the grains in oil. Add the broth, salt, and oregano and cook, stirring, for another 30 seconds.

3. (If using a skillet, transfer the ingredients to the pressure cooker at this point.) Add the chicken to the cooker. Bring the pressure to high (15 psi) and cook for 15 minutes. Use the Natural Release method.

4. As soon as possible, remove the chicken and rice to a large platter. Add the peas and minced parsley to the top. Tent the platter with aluminum foil for at least 5 minutes, allowing the peas to steam to doneness. Remove the foil, sprinkle the lime juice on top, and serve immediately.

Brown Rice with Vegetables

SERVES 4

PRESSURE TIMING: 10 MINUTES

Healthful and a cinch to make, this recipe should become a go-to staple in your pressure cooking repertoire, especially if you have an eye to health. Change out the vegetables as you like, using those that you like best in this dish.

1½ CUPS WATER

1 CUP MEDIUM-GRAIN BROWN RICE

2 OUNCES SLICED BLANCHED ALMONDS

1 CUP CHOPPED FRESH OR CANNED TOMATOES

½ CUP CHOPPED CARROT

½ CUP CHOPPED CELERY

½ CUP CHOPPED RED BELL PEPPER

Pour the water into the bottom of the pressure cooker. Combine the rice, almonds, and vegetables in a metal bowl and place the bowl on the rack inside the cooker. Bring the pressure to high (15 psi) and cook for 10 minutes. Use the Natural Release method. Fluff the rice with a fork and serve.

Basic Risotto

SERVES 4

PRESSURE TIMING: 8 MINUTES

A pressure cooker makes delicious risotto without requiring you to stir a hot pan for 20 minutes. Here, it's just a quick sauté and 8 minutes in the cooker. The higher-quality broth or stock you use—ideally one you make yourself, such as Homemade Chicken Broth on page 90—the better your risotto.

2 TABLESPOONS OLIVE OIL

1 ONION, CHOPPED

2 CUPS ARBORIO RICE

2 TABLESPOONS DRY WHITE WINE

4 CUPS REDUCED-SODIUM CHICKEN OR VEGETABLE BROTH

1 TO 2 TABLESPOONS UNSALTED BUTTER

GRATED PARMESAN CHEESE

CHOPPED FRESH PARSLEY, FOR GARNISH

1. In the bottom of the pressure cooker or in a skillet on the stove top, heat the oil over medium-high heat. Add the onion and sauté until translucent, about 5 minutes.

2. Add the rice to the onion and stir, coating it with the oil. When the grains start to turn color, add the wine. Continue to cook, scraping up the browned bits on the inside of the pan. Add the broth and continue to stir.

3. (If using a skillet, transfer the ingredients to the pressure cooker at this point.) Bring the pressure to high (15 psi) and cook for 8 minutes. Use the Natural Release method.

4. Stir in the butter and add Parmesan cheese to taste. Sprinkle the parsley on top and serve.

Shrimp Risotto

SERVES 4

PRESSURE TIMING: 10 MINUTES

Shrimp is the star attraction in this pressure cooker risotto recipe, in which the rice is cooked in the cooker and the dish completed on the stove top.

2 TABLESPOONS UNSALTED BUTTER, DIVIDED

1 ONION, DICED

3 GARLIC CLOVES, MINCED

1½ CUPS ARBORIO RICE

4 CUPS REDUCED-SODIUM CHICKEN OR VEGETABLE BROTH, DIVIDED

SALT AND GROUND BLACK PEPPER

1 POUND SHRIMP, PEELED AND DEVEINED

½ CUP GRATED PARMESAN CHEESE

¼ CUP CHOPPED FRESH BASIL

¼ CUP CHOPPED FRESH PARSLEY

1. In the bottom of the pressure cooker or in a skillet on the stove top, melt 1 tablespoon of the butter. Sauté the onion and garlic until translucent, about 5 minutes. Stir in the rice, coating it with the oil. Continue cooking until the rice goes from white to translucent, with a little toasted brown.

2. Combine the rice and 3 cups of the broth in the pressure cooker and season with salt and pepper. Bring the pressure to high (15 psi) and cook for 10 minutes. Use the Natural Release method.

3. Transfer the contents of the pressure cooker to a skillet if necessary and stir in the remaining 1 tablespoon butter, 1 cup broth, and the shrimp. Stir the risotto over high heat on the stove top until the shrimp turns light pink, about 3 minutes. Add the cheese and most of the basil and parsley and toss. Serve immediately with a sprinkle of the remaining herbs.

Mushroom-Parmesan Risotto

SERVES 4

PRESSURE TIMING: 10 MINUTES

Serve this risotto at your next small dinner party, and don't tell anyone how easy it was to make. A mixture of exotic mushrooms makes this dish even more elegant.

2 TABLESPOONS UNSALTED BUTTER, DIVIDED

1 ONION, DICED

2 GARLIC CLOVES, MINCED

1 CUP SLICED MIXED MUSHROOMS (SUCH AS BUTTON, CREMINI, AND CHANTERELLE)

PINCH OF SUGAR

PINCH OF SALT

2 CUPS ARBORIO RICE

4 CUPS REDUCED-SODIUM CHICKEN OR VEGETABLE BROTH

¼ CUP GRATED PARMESAN CHEESE

1. In the bottom of the pressure cooker or in a skillet on the stove top, melt 1 tablespoon of the butter over medium-high heat. Add the onion and garlic and sauté until translucent, about 5 minutes. Add the mushrooms, sugar, and salt, and stir until the mushrooms are softened and begin to give up their moisture. Add the rice and stir until the grains are coated with butter and some are beginning to turn golden.

2. Combine the rice-mushroom mixture and the broth in the pressure cooker; bring the pressure to high (15 psi) and cook for 10 minutes. Use the Quick Release method. Stir in the remaining tablespoon of butter and the cheese. Serve immediately.

Asparagus-Leek Risotto

SERVES 4

PRESSURE TIMING: 10 MINUTES

This risotto makes a perfect accompaniment to a dinner of roasted meat or fish and a salad. Or, for a vegan entrée, stir in ½-inch squares of tofu after cooking. For best results, use the thinnest asparagus you can find.

2 TABLESPOONS UNSALTED BUTTER, DIVIDED

2 TABLESPOONS OLIVE OIL

1½ CUPS THINLY SLICED LEEKS

3 GARLIC CLOVES, MINCED

1½ CUPS ARBORIO RICE

4 CUPS VEGETABLE BROTH

½ POUND THIN ASPARAGUS, CUT INTO 1-INCH PIECES

1 CUP GRATED PARMESAN

1. In the bottom of the pressure cooker or in a skillet on the stove top, melt 1 tablespoon of the butter in the oil. Add the leeks and garlic and cook, stirring frequently, for about 5 minutes. Add the rice and stir until the grains are coated with fat and some are beginning to turn golden.

2. Combine the rice-leek mixture and the vegetable broth in the pressure cooker; bring the pressure to high (15 psi) and cook for 10 minutes. Use the Quick Release method.

3. While the rice cooks, steam the asparagus in a rack set over a pot of boiling water until just tender.

4. After releasing the pressure, stir the steamed asparagus and cheese into the risotto. Add the remaining tablespoon of butter and stir again until the butter melts. Serve.

CHAPTER SIX

Pasta

Simple Tomato Sauce

SERVES 4

PRESSURE TIMING: 45 MINUTES

This simple, rustic sauce tastes as though it's been simmering all day, but it takes just 45 minutes in the pressure cooker. It is perfect with light pastas such as angel hair, or served in a heaping spoonful alongside a piece of grilled fish.

2 LARGE ONIONS, CUT INTO QUARTERS

3 CARROTS, PEELED AND CUT INTO CHUNKS

5 GARLIC CLOVES, PEELED AND HALVED

3 TABLESPOONS EXTRA-VIRGIN OLIVE OIL, DIVIDED

SALT

ONE 28-OUNCE CAN CRUSHED TOMATOES

¼ CUP CHOPPED FRESH BASIL OR PARSLEY, OR A COMBINATION

1 TABLESPOON BALSAMIC VINEGAR (OPTIONAL)

1. In a food processor, combine the onions, carrots, and garlic and pulse until finely minced.

2. In the bottom of the pressure cooker or in a large skillet on the stove top, heat 2 tablespoons of the oil over medium-high heat. Add the minced vegetables and cook, stirring, until the vegetables are soft, 3 to 5 minutes. Season with salt.

3. Combine the sautéed vegetables and tomatoes in the pressure cooker; bring the pressure to high (15 psi) and cook for 45 minutes. Use the Natural Release method. Stir in the herbs, the remaining tablespoon of olive oil, and the vinegar, if using. Serve.

Farfalle with Tomato Sauce

SERVES 4

PRESSURE TIMING: 6 MINUTES

Dried pasta cooks on low pressure in the pressure cooker in about half the time it takes to cook on the stove top—and you don't have to wait for a big pot of water to boil. This is a great starter recipe; add browned ground beef or turkey, fresh tomatoes, more herbs, or anything else you'd like to jazz it up.

2 TABLESPOONS VEGETABLE OIL

3 GARLIC CLOVES, MINCED

1 TEASPOON RED PEPPER FLAKES

1 TEASPOON DRIED OREGANO

1 POUND FARFALLE

ONE 14.5-OUNCE CAN TOMATO PURÉE

2 TEASPOONS SALT

WATER

¼ CUP GRATED PARMESAN OR ROMANO CHEESE

1. In the bottom of the pressure cooker or in a skillet on the stove top, heat the oil over medium heat. Add the garlic, pepper flakes, and oregano and stir for 1 minute.

2. Combine the seasoned oil, pasta, tomato purée, and salt in the pressure cooker and add just enough water to cover the ingredients. Mix thoroughly. Bring the pressure to low (8 psi) and cook for 6 minutes. Use the Quick Release method. Serve immediately with the grated cheese.

Quick Rigatoni Casserole

SERVES 4–6

TIMING PRESSURE: 5 MINUTES

This pasta casserole makes a great family meal any night of the week. It is cooked on low pressure and finished under the broiler to melt the cheese.

2 TABLESPOONS OLIVE OIL

1 POUND LEAN GROUND BEEF

1 ONION, CHOPPED

2 TO 3 TABLESPOONS DRY RED WINE

1 CARROT, PEELED AND CHOPPED

1 CELERY STALK, CHOPPED

1 POUND RIGATONI

ONE 14.5-OUNCE CAN TOMATO PURÉE

WATER

3 OUNCES GRATED PARMESAN CHEESE

¼ CUP CHOPPED FRESH BASIL OR PARSLEY, OR A COMBINATION

1. In the bottom of the pressure cooker or in a skillet on the stove top, heat the oil over medium-high heat until it shines, then add the ground beef and onion. Cook until the onion is soft, 5 to 7 minutes. Add the red wine and simmer for 2 minutes. Add the carrot and celery and cook for another 5 minutes.

2. Preheat the broiler.

3. Combine the ground beef mixture, rigatoni, and tomato purée in the pressure cooker and add just enough water to cover the ingredients. Bring the pressure to low (8 psi) and cook for 5 minutes. Use the Quick Release method.

4. Pour the contents of the pressure cooker into a casserole pan and sprinkle the cheese over the top. Slide under the broiler until the cheese is melted and bubbly. Sprinkle the chopped fresh herbs over the casserole and serve.

Spaghetti with Bolognese Sauce

SERVES 4
PRESSURE TIMING: 20 MINUTES

Cook the pasta on the stove top while the sauce works its magic in the pressure cooker. This sauce has the same deep, complicated flavors as one that has simmered all day.

2 TABLESPOONS OLIVE OIL

1 POUND LEAN GROUND BEEF

2 ONIONS, CHOPPED

3 GARLIC CLOVES, MINCED

½ CUP TOMATO PASTE

½ CUP REDUCED-SODIUM BEEF BROTH

ONE 14.5-OUNCE CAN CRUSHED TOMATOES

1 TABLESPOON BALSAMIC VINEGAR

DRIED HERBS

SALT

1 POUND SPAGHETTI

1. In the bottom of the pressure cooker or in a skillet on the stove top, heat the oil over medium-high heat until shiny. Add the beef and cook until no longer pink. Add the onions and garlic and cook until soft, about 3 minutes.

2. Combine the beef mixture, tomato paste, beef broth, crushed tomatoes, vinegar, dried herbs, and salt in the pressure cooker. Bring the pressure to high (15 psi) and cook for 20 minutes. Use the Natural Release method.

3. While the sauce is cooking, bring a large pot of water to a boil over high heat. Add the spaghetti and cook until al dente according to the package instructions. Drain.

4. If the sauce is too watery, simmer it, uncovered, on the stove top until thick. Serve immediately over the spaghetti.

Pork Ragu on Egg Noodles

SERVES 4

PRESSURE TIMING: 8 MINUTES

This rustic sauce particularly complements the flavor of egg noodles. Serve with a hearty red wine.

¼ CUP DICED PANCETTA

2 POUNDS PORK STEW MEAT, CUT INTO 1-INCH CUBES

1 ONION, CHOPPED

2 CARROTS, PEELED AND CHOPPED

3 GARLIC CLOVES, MINCED

1 CUP DRY RED WINE

ONE 15-OUNCE CAN TOMATO SAUCE

2 TEASPOONS DRIED OREGANO

1 TEASPOON DRIED BASIL

¾ POUNDS EGG NOODLES

1. In the bottom of the pressure cooker or in a skillet on the stove top, sauté the pancetta and pork over high heat until the pancetta gives up its fat and the pork browns. Add the onion, carrots, and garlic and sauté for 3 minutes. Add the wine and simmer for 3 minutes, scraping up any browned bits from the bottom.

2. Combine the pork mixture with the tomato sauce, oregano, and basil in the pressure cooker. Bring the pressure to high (15 psi) and cook for 8 minutes. Use the Natural Release method.

3. While the ragu cooks, bring a large pot of water to a boil over high heat. Add the egg noodles and cook until al dente according to the package instructions. Drain.

4. Divide the noodles among four plates and top with the pork ragu. Serve immediately.

Pasta and Chickpeas (*Pasta e Ceci*)

SERVES 4

PRESSURE TIMING: 14 MINUTES

The Italians are known for serving pasta and beans together, as in this delicious, soupy bowl of pasta and ceci (chickpeas). Add a sprinkling of grated cheese on top and serve with chunks of warm bread. It's heaven.

2 TABLESPOONS OLIVE OIL

1 ONION, CHOPPED

1 CELERY STALK, CHOPPED

2 GARLIC CLOVES, MINCED

1 CUP DRIED CHICKPEAS, SOAKED (PAGE 8) AND DRAINED

1 CUP DITALINI OR OTHER SMALL PASTA

4 CUPS WATER

2 TABLESPOONS TOMATO PASTE

½ TEASPOON DRIED ROSEMARY

½ TEASPOON DRIED SAGE

SALT AND GROUND BLACK PEPPER

1. In the bottom of the pressure cooker or in a skillet on the stove top, heat the oil over high heat until it shines. Add the onion, celery, and garlic and cook until softened, about 5 minutes.

2. Combine the onion mixture with the chickpeas, pasta, water, tomato paste, rosemary, and sage in the pressure cooker. Bring the pressure to high (15 psi) and cook for 14 minutes. Use the Natural Release method. Season with salt and pepper and serve immediately.

Macaroni and Cheese

SERVES 4

PRESSURE TIMING: 4 MINUTES

This mac and cheese is cheesy and creamy, the way everyone likes it. For extra deliciousness, throw bite-sized chunks of ham or lobster meat in just before the trip to the broiler.

1 POUND ELBOW MACARONI

3 TABLESPOONS UNSALTED BUTTER, DIVIDED

1 TABLESPOON YELLOW MUSTARD

1½ TEASPOONS SALT

1 TEASPOON HOT PEPPER SAUCE

WATER

1½ CUPS (12 OUNCES) SHREDDED EXTRA SHARP CHEDDAR CHEESE

1 CUP PANKO BREAD CRUMBS

¾ CUP (6 OUNCES) SHREDDED PARMESAN CHEESE

1. Preheat the broiler.

2. Combine the macaroni, 2 tablespoons of the butter, the mustard, salt, and hot pepper sauce in the pressure cooker. Add just enough water to cover the ingredients; bring the pressure to high (15 psi) and cook for 4 minutes. Use the Quick Release method.

3. Immediately start adding the Cheddar cheese by the handful, stirring until all of the cheese is melted and integrated.

4. Pour the contents of the pressure cooker into a casserole pan. Sprinkle the panko crumbs over the top, followed by the Parmesan cheese. Broil until the cheeses are bubbly and hot, 3 to 4 minutes. Serve immediately.

One-Pot Mexican Macaroni

SERVES 4

PRESSURE TIMING: 6 MINUTES

It's hard to go wrong with Mexican food, and this south-of-the-border take on pasta is no exception. With minimal preparation and a fast cooking time, this is a great weeknight meal for a busy, hungry family.

2 TABLESPOONS OLIVE OIL

1 POUND LEAN GROUND BEEF

1 RED OR GREEN BELL PEPPER, SEEDED AND CHOPPED

1 ONION, CHOPPED

ONE 15-OUNCE CAN PINTO BEANS, RINSED AND DRAINED

ONE 10-OUNCE CAN DICED TOMATOES WITH GREEN CHILES, DRAINED

ONE 8-OUNCE CAN TOMATO SAUCE

2 CUPS ELBOW MACARONI

WATER

¾ CUP (6 OUNCES) SHREDDED MONTEREY JACK CHEESE

1. In the bottom of the pressure cooker or in a skillet on the stove top, heat the oil over medium-high heat. Add the ground beef and sauté until no longer pink. Pour off as much liquid as possible. Add the bell pepper and onion and cook, stirring often, until the vegetables soften, 6 to 8 minutes.

2. Combine the ground beef mixture, beans, tomatoes with chiles, tomato sauce, and macaroni in the pressure cooker and add just enough water to cover the ingredients. Bring the pressure to high (15 psi) and cook for 6 minutes. Use the Natural Release method. Immediately stir in the cheese and serve.

Ziti and Italian Sausages

SERVES 4

PRESSURE TIMING: 5 MINUTES

Tube-shaped ziti is a great pairing with the flavorful Italian sausage used in this recipe. This easy-to-make dish is very satisfying on its own, or serve it with your favorite steamed vegetables to lend depth.

2 TABLESPOONS OLIVE OIL

1 POUND SWEET OR HOT ITALIAN SAUSAGE, REMOVED FROM CASINGS

1 ONION, CHOPPED

1 RED OR GREEN BELL PEPPER, SEEDED AND CHOPPED

ONE 24-OUNCE JAR TOMATO SAUCE

3½ CUPS WATER

1 POUND ZITI

¼ CUP CHOPPED FRESH BASIL

SALT AND GROUND BLACK PEPPER

1. In the bottom of the pressure cooker or in a skillet on the stove top, heat the oil over medium-high heat until it shines. Add the sausage meat, onion, and bell pepper and cook, stirring frequently, until the meat is no longer pink. Drain off the fat.

2. Combine the sausage mixture with the tomato sauce, water, and ziti in the pressure cooker. Bring the pressure to high (15 psi) and cook for 5 minutes. Use the Quick Release method.

3. If the ziti is not quite al dente, allow the stew to simmer for a minute or two on the stove top (transfer to a large stockpot if necessary). Stir in the basil, season with salt and pepper, and serve immediately.

Fusilli with Spinach

SERVES 4

PRESSURE TIMING: 5 MINUTES

Here, spinach and pasta are combined in a pressure cooker, with extra-virgin olive oil swirled in at the end. The flavors are subtle and smooth.

1 POUND FRESH SPINACH (OR FROZEN, THAWED AND
    SQUEEZED OF LIQUID)
4 GARLIC CLOVES, MINCED
1 POUND FUSILLI
1½ TEASPOONS SALT
WATER
1 TABLESPOON EXTRA-VIRGIN OLIVE OIL

1. In the bottom of the pressure cooker or in a skillet on the stove top, cook the spinach and garlic over medium heat until the spinach's moisture has evaporated.

2. Combine the spinach, fusilli, and salt in the pressure cooker and add just enough water to cover the ingredients. Bring the pressure to low (8 psi) and cook for 5 minutes. Use the Quick Release method. Stir in the olive oil and serve immediately.

CHAPTER SEVEN

Seafood

Seafood Lover's Stew

SERVES 4

PRESSURE TIMING: 10 MINUTES

This stew builds huge flavor with a roux prepared on the stove top, followed by just 10 minutes in the pressure cooker. Serve with a garden salad and crusty bread.

2 TABLESPOONS UNSALTED BUTTER

2 TABLESPOONS FLOUR

1 CUP DRY WHITE WINE

1 ONION, CHOPPED

4 TO 5 GARLIC CLOVES, MINCED

2 TOMATOES, CHOPPED

3 CELERY STALKS, THINLY SLICED

ONE 24-OUNCE JAR TOMATO SAUCE

1 CUP REDUCED-SODIUM CHICKEN BROTH

2 CUPS OF ANY OF THE FOLLOWING, OR A COMBINATION: PEELED AND DEVEINED SHRIMP, SCALLOPS, CLAMS, MUSSELS, SALMON CHUNKS, CALAMARI RINGS

½ TEASPOON CRUMBLED SAFFRON STRANDS

1. In the bottom of the pressure cooker or in a skillet on the stove top, melt the butter over medium heat. Add the flour and stir it into the butter until it darkens slightly. Add the white wine and continue stirring. When the roux is thick, add the onion, garlic, tomatoes, and celery. Continue stirring for 3 to 4 minutes.

2. Combine the vegetable-roux mixture, tomato sauce, broth, seafood, and saffron in the pressure cooker. The cooker should be no more than two-thirds full. Bring the pressure to high (15 psi) and cook for 10 minutes. Use the Natural Release method. Serve immediately.

Mediterranean-Style Fish Fillets

SERVES 4

PRESSURE TIMING: 5 MINUTES

Simple, fast, and fresh tasting, this dish feels like dinner on the beach.

1 PINT CHERRY TOMATOES, HALVED

1 FRESH THYME SPRIG

4 WHITE FISH FILLETS (SUCH AS SNAPPER, HALIBUT, SOLE, OR TILAPIA),
RINSED AND PATTED DRY

1 CUP SALT-CURED BLACK OLIVES (SUCH AS KALAMATA)

3 TABLESPOONS CAPERS, DRAINED

1. Place the tomato halves in a metal bowl that fits inside the pressure cooker. Place the thyme on top of the tomatoes, lay the fish on the thyme, and top with the olives and capers. Set the bowl on the rack in the pressure cooker; bring the pressure to high (15 psi) and cook for 5 minutes. Use the Quick Release method.

2. Place one fish fillet on each of four plates and spoon the tomato-olive-caper mixture on top. Serve immediately.

Seafood Gumbo

SERVES 4
PRESSURE TIMING: 1 MINUTE

All the work of this recipe is in the prep—once in the cooker, it's ready in just one minute. You can prepare the rice on the stove top or cook it in your pressure cooker (page 6) before making the gumbo.

1 POUND SHRIMP, PEELED AND DEVEINED

1 POUND SOLE FILLETS, CUT INTO 2-INCH PIECES

2½ CUPS REDUCED-SODIUM CHICKEN BROTH

ONE 14.5-OUNCE CAN DICED TOMATOES, DRAINED

1 CUP CHOPPED ONION

1 CUP CHOPPED RED OR GREEN BELL PEPPER

2 TABLESPOONS DRIED PARSLEY

1 TABLESPOON DRIED BASIL

½ TEASPOON DRIED THYME

½ TEASPOON CAYENNE PEPPER

½ TEASPOON SALT

¼ CUP COLD WATER

2 TABLESPOONS CORNSTARCH

ONE 10-OUNCE PACKAGE FROZEN SLICED OKRA, THAWED

COOKED WHITE RICE, FOR SERVING

1. Combine the shrimp, sole, broth, tomatoes, onion, bell pepper, parsley, basil, thyme, cayenne, and salt in the pressure cooker. Bring the pressure to high (15 psi) and cook for 1 minute. Use the Quick Release method.

2. In a small bowl, whisk together the cold water and cornstarch. Slowly add the cornstarch mixture to the gumbo and stir constantly until it thickens. Stir in the thawed okra. Serve immediately with bowls of rice.

Jambalaya

SERVES 4

PRESSURE TIMING: 8 MINUTES

This bold Creole classic will make anyone want to celebrate. Feel free to experiment with different ingredients for this one-pot dish, adding different types of sausage (smoked or fully cooked) or fish fillets cut into 1-inch chunks.

2 TABLESPOONS VEGETABLE OIL

½ POUND SHRIMP, PEELED AND DEVEINED

½ CUP 1-INCH CUBED BONELESS CHICKEN BREASTS

½ POUND ANDOUILLE SAUSAGE, SLICED

2 TEASPOONS CREOLE SEASONING, DIVIDED

1 ONION, CHOPPED

4 GARLIC CLOVES, MINCED

1 CUP CHOPPED RED OR GREEN BELL PEPPER

2 CELERY STALKS, THINLY SLICED

1 TEASPOON DRIED THYME

¼ TEASPOON CAYENNE PEPPER

ONE 14.5-OUNCE CAN DICED TOMATOES, DRAINED

1 CUP LONG-GRAIN WHITE RICE

1 CUP REDUCED-SODIUM CHICKEN BROTH

¼ CUP CHOPPED FRESH PARSLEY, TO SERVE

1. In the bottom of the pressure cooker or in a skillet on the stove top, heat the oil over medium-high heat until the oil shines. Add the shrimp, chicken, and sausage and sprinkle 1 teaspoon of the Creole seasoning over the meats. Sauté until the shrimp and chicken are cooked through, 3 to 5 minutes. Remove the meats to a plate and set aside.

2. Add the onion, garlic, bell pepper, celery, thyme, cayenne, and the remaining teaspoon of Creole seasoning to the skillet and sauté until the vegetables are soft, 4 to 5 minutes.

continued ▶

3. Combine the vegetables, tomatoes, rice, and broth in the pressure cooker; bring the pressure to high (15 psi) and cook for 8 minutes. Use the Quick Release method.

4. Stir the meats into the stew and mix thoroughly. Transfer to a serving bowl and sprinkle the parsley over the top. Serve immediately.

Steamed Salmon

SERVES 2

PRESSURE TIMING: 6 MINUTES

Here's a light yet flavorful idea for dinner. This recipe is easily doubled; just don't fill the cooker more than two-thirds full.

1 TABLESPOON BROWN SUGAR

1 TABLESPOON SALT

2 TABLESPOONS UNSALTED BUTTER, AT ROOM TEMPERATURE

TWO 10- TO 12-OUNCE SALMON FILLETS

1 CUP WATER, DRY WHITE WINE, OR FISH STOCK

½ LEMON, THINLY SLICED

In a small bowl, mix the brown sugar and salt. Spread the butter over the fillets, then sprinkle the sugar-salt mixture over them. Pour the liquid into the bottom of the pressure cooker, set the rack in the pot, and lay the fillets on the rack. Arrange the lemon slices on top of the fillets. Bring the pressure to high (15 psi) and cook for 6 minutes. Use the Quick Release method. Serve immediately.

Shrimp with Snow Peas

Faster than a drive-through, this delightful dish is full of fresh flavors. Serve over rice or udon noodles.

1 POUND SHRIMP, PEELED AND DEVEINED

½ POUND SNOW PEAS

3 TABLESPOONS REDUCED-SODIUM SOY SAUCE

2 TABLESPOONS VINEGAR

1 TABLESPOON SUGAR

1 CUP REDUCED-SODIUM CHICKEN BROTH

¼ CUP CHOPPED FRESH PARSLEY

Combine the shrimp, snow peas, soy sauce, vinegar, sugar, and broth in the pressure cooker. Bring the pressure to high (15 psi) and cook for 3 minutes. Use the Quick Release method. Transfer to a serving bowl, sprinkle the parsley on top, and serve.

Coconut Fish Curry

SERVES 4

PRESSURE TIMING: 3 MINUTES

Serve this healthy, delicious stew over rice or grains for a chic lunch or dinner.

2 TABLESPOONS OLIVE OIL

2 ONIONS, THINLY SLICED AND SEPARATED INTO RINGS

3 GARLIC CLOVES, MINCED

1 TABLESPOON GRATED FRESH GINGER

3 TABLESPOONS CURRY POWDER

1½ POUNDS WHITE FISH FILLETS (SUCH AS SNAPPER, HALIBUT, SOLE, OR
    TILAPIA), CUT INTO 1-INCH PIECES

ONE 14-OUNCE CAN COCONUT MILK

JUICE OF ½ LEMON

1 TO 2 TEASPOONS SALT

1. In the bottom of the pressure cooker or in a skillet on the stove top, heat the oil over medium-high heat. Add the onion rings and cook until soft, 6 to 8 minutes. Add the garlic and cook for 2 minutes. Add the ginger and curry powder and cook for another minute.

2. Combine the onion mixture, fish, coconut milk, lemon juice, and salt in the pressure cooker. Bring the pressure to high (15 psi) and cook for 3 minutes. Use the Natural Release method. Serve immediately.

Haddock in Cheese Sauce

SERVES 4

PRESSURE TIMING: 5 MINUTES

Haddock has a fine, clean flavor similar to cod. The cheese sauce in this recipe is cooked on the stove top, and the dish is finished in 5 minutes in the pressure cooker. This dish pairs well with rice, grains, or pasta.

2 TABLESPOONS UNSALTED BUTTER

2 TABLESPOONS FLOUR

½ TEASPOON SALT

1 CUP MILK

2 CUPS (16 OUNCES) SHREDDED CHEDDAR OR MONTEREY JACK CHEESE

2 POUNDS HADDOCK FILLETS

1½ CUPS WATER

1. In a medium saucepan, melt the butter over medium heat. Add the flour and salt and whisk to blend. Slowly pour in the milk, whisking constantly, until thick. Add the cheese and stir until it has melted into the sauce.

2. Lay the haddock fillets in a metal bowl that fits inside the pressure cooker. Pour the cheese sauce over the fish. Cover the bowl with aluminum foil. Pour the water into the bottom of the pressure cooker and place the bowl on the rack in the cooker. Bring the pressure to high (15 psi) and cook for 5 minutes. Use the Quick Release method. Serve immediately.

Almond Cod

SERVES 4

PRESSURE TIMING: 2 MINUTES

Lightly perfumed with almonds, garlic, and herbs, this fish cooks to perfection in just 2 minutes. Cod is low in saturated fat and a great source of omega-3s, vitamins, and minerals.

1 TABLESPOON VEGETABLE OIL

4 TABLESPOONS SLICED ALMONDS, DIVIDED

3 GARLIC CLOVES, HALVED

½ CUP FRESH PARSLEY LEAVES

1 TEASPOON DRIED OREGANO

½ TEASPOON PAPRIKA

1 POUND COD FILLETS

1 CUP REDUCED-SODIUM CHICKEN BROTH

1. In a small sauté pan, heat the oil over medium-high heat. Add 2 tablespoons of the almonds and cook, stirring frequently, until the almonds are golden brown. Remove and set aside to drain on paper towels.

2. In a food processor, pulse the garlic, parsley, oregano, paprika, and remaining 2 tablespoons almonds until the ingredients form a paste. Slather the paste on the cod fillets. Put the fillets in a metal bowl that fits inside the pressure cooker. Cover the bowl with aluminum foil.

3. Pour the chicken broth into the pressure cooker. Place the bowl on the rack in the pressure cooker. Bring the pressure to high (15 psi) and cook for 2 minutes. Use the Quick Release method. Sprinkle the browned almonds over the top and serve.

Raspberry Salmon

SERVES 4

PRESSURE TIMING: 3 MINUTES

Marinating the salmon before cooking gives it a whisper of tangy raspberry flavor that complements the rich fish.

4 SALMON STEAKS, ABOUT 1 INCH THICK

2 CUPS RASPBERRY VINEGAR

2 TABLESPOONS VEGETABLE OIL

4 LEEKS, WHITE PARTS ONLY, THINLY SLICED

3 GARLIC CLOVES, MINCED

3 TABLESPOONS CHOPPED FRESH PARSLEY

1 CUP CLAM JUICE

2 TABLESPOONS FRESH LEMON JUICE

1 TEASPOON SALT

¼ CUP CHOPPED FRESH DILL, DIVIDED

1. Place the salmon steaks in a large zip-top plastic bag and pour in the raspberry vinegar. Toss to coat. Marinate in the refrigerator for 2 hours.

2. In the bottom of the pressure cooker or in a skillet on the stove top, heat the oil over medium-high heat until shiny. Add the leeks, garlic, and parsley and cook, stirring, until the leeks are soft, about 3 minutes. Add the clam juice, lemon juice, salt, and 2 tablespoons of the dill. Stir and cook for 1 minute.

3. (If using a skillet, transfer the contents to the pressure cooker at this point.) Remove the salmon steaks from the vinegar (discard the vinegar) and add them to the mixture, turning to coat the fish.

4. Bring the pressure to high (15 psi) and cook for 3 minutes. Use the Quick Release method. Remove the fish to a serving platter, spoon the vegetables over the fish, and sprinkle with the remaining dill. Serve immediately.

CHAPTER EIGHT

Poultry

Whole Chicken

SERVES 4-6

PRESSURE TIMING: 25 MINUTES

New generations are discovering what our grandparents and great-grandparents knew: a whole chicken cooks perfectly in the pressure cooker. This recipe is also the beginning of many great dishes: chicken salad, chicken soup, chicken pot pie, or any recipe that calls for delicious chunks of perfect chicken. If you are using the meat for another dish, you can skip browning the bird.

ONE 3 1/2- TO 4-POUND CHICKEN

SALT AND GROUND BLACK PEPPER

2 TABLESPOONS VEGETABLE OIL

1½ CUPS REDUCED-SODIUM CHICKEN BROTH OR WATER

1. Season the chicken all over with salt and pepper. In the bottom of the pressure cooker or in a large skillet on the stove top, heat the oil over medium-high heat. Brown the chicken on all sides.

2. Put the rack in the bottom of the pressure cooker. Pour the broth into the cooker and set the chicken on the rack. Bring the pressure to high (15 psi) and cook for 25 minutes. Use the Quick Release method. Serve immediately, or let it cool before pulling the meat off the bones for use in another dish.

Whole Chicken with Vegetables

SERVES 4-6

PRESSURE TIMING: 25 MINUTES

Chicken cooked this way is wonderful served over rice, couscous, or mashed potatoes.

ONE 3½- TO 4-POUND CHICKEN

SALT AND GROUND BLACK PEPPER

2 TABLESPOONS VEGETABLE OIL

1 ONION, CHOPPED

2 GARLIC CLOVES, MINCED (OPTIONAL)

3 CELERY STALKS, THINLY SLICED

1½ CUPS REDUCED-SODIUM CHICKEN BROTH OR WATER

1 CUP BABY CARROTS OR 1-INCH CARROT PIECES

1. Season the chicken all over with salt and pepper. In the bottom of the pressure cooker or in a large skillet on the stove top, heat the oil over medium-high heat. Brown the chicken on all sides. Remove to a plate and set aside.

2. Add the onion, garlic (if using), and celery to the skillet and sauté over high heat until soft, 5 to 7 minutes.

3. Put the rack in the bottom of the pressure cooker. Pour the broth into the cooker and set the chicken on the rack. Spoon the sautéed vegetables and add carrots around the chicken. Bring the pressure to high (15 psi) and cook for 25 minutes. Use the Quick Release method.

4. Transfer the chicken to a serving platter. Arrange the vegetables around it and spoon the chicken juices over all. Serve immediately.

Homemade Chicken Broth

MAKES ABOUT 8 CUPS

PRESSURE TIMING: 30 MINUTES

Use the chicken carcass left over from any of the whole chicken recipes in this book (pages 88, 89, 91, and 97) to create the base for delicious one-pot meals, soups, and stews. Store the broth in covered containers in the refrigerator for up to 3 days or in the freezer for up to 6 months.

1 COOKED CHICKEN CARCASS (BONES WITH BITS OF MEAT)

8 CUPS WATER

2 ONIONS, HALVED

1 CELERY STALK, CUT INTO CHUNKS

2 MEDIUM CARROTS, SCRUBBED AND CUT INTO CHUNKS

1 BUNCH FRESH PARSLEY

4 FRESH THYME SPRIGS OR 1 TEASPOON DRIED THYME

2 GARLIC CLOVES, HALVED

1 TABLESPOON BLACK PEPPERCORNS

1. Combine all of the ingredients in the pressure cooker; bring the pressure to high (15 psi) and cook for 30 minutes. Use the Quick Release method.

2. Remove the chicken carcass and pour the remaining contents of the pressure cooker through a mesh strainer into a large bowl or pot. Use immediately in another dish or store for later use.

Chicken with Potatoes and Peas

SERVES 4–6

PRESSURE TIMING: 30 MINUTES, DIVIDED

This recipe calls for a whole chicken, which takes just 25 minutes to cook in a pressure cooker. Cook the potatoes in the juices from the chicken, a time-honored and glorious way to cook potatoes.

ONE 3½- TO 4-POUND CHICKEN
SALT AND GROUND BLACK PEPPER
2 TABLESPOONS VEGETABLE OIL
1½ CUPS REDUCED-SODIUM CHICKEN BROTH OR WATER
WATER
2 LARGE POTATOES, THINLY SLICED
ONE 10-OUNCE PACKAGE FROZEN PEAS

1. Season the chicken all over with salt and pepper. In the bottom of the pressure cooker or in a large skillet on the stove top, heat the oil over medium-high heat. Brown the chicken on all sides.

2. Put the rack in the bottom of the pressure cooker. Pour the broth into the cooker and set the chicken on the rack. Bring the pressure to high (15 psi) and cook for 25 minutes. Use the Quick Release method. Remove the chicken from the cooker and place on a serving platter. Tent with aluminum foil to keep warm.

3. Measure the liquid at the bottom of the pressure cooker and add enough water to make 2½ cups. Add the potatoes and toss them in the chicken drippings. Bring the pressure to high (15 psi) and cook for 5 minutes. Use the Quick Release method.

4. Immediately add the frozen peas to the pressure cooker. Close the lid (but do not seal) and let the peas steam for 3 minutes. Spoon the potatoes and peas around the chicken on the serving platter and serve.

Chicken with Olives

SERVES 4–6

PRESSURE TIMING: 8 MINUTES

You can substitute briny green olives in this recipe, if you'd like. Serve on a platter along with a large bowl of rice or grains of your choosing.

JUICE OF 3 LEMONS

3 GARLIC CLOVES, MINCED

½ CUP CHOPPED PARSLEY

2 TABLESPOONS CHOPPED FRESH ROSEMARY

2 FRESH SAGE LEAVES, CHOPPED

ONE 3½- TO 4-POUND CHICKEN, CUT INTO 8 PIECES

2 TABLESPOONS VEGETABLE OIL

½ CUP DRY WHITE WINE

½ CUP BLACK SALT-CURED OLIVES (SUCH AS KALAMATA)

THIN LEMON SLICES, FOR GARNISH (OPTIONAL)

1. In a large zip-top plastic bag, combine the lemon juice, garlic, parsley, rosemary, and sage. Add the chicken pieces and toss to coat. Let marinate in the refrigerator for at least 2 hours.

2. In the bottom of the pressure cooker or in a large skillet on the stove top, heat the oil over medium-high heat. Remove the chicken pieces from the marinade (reserve the marinade) and add to the skillet, in batches if necessary. Brown the chicken pieces, turning once, about 4 minutes.

3. Combine the marinade and white wine in the bottom of the pressure cooker. Add the chicken pieces. Bring the pressure to high (15 psi) and cook for 8 minutes. Use the Natural Release method.

4. Arrange the chicken pieces on a large serving platter. Sprinkle the olives over the chicken and garnish with thin lemon slices, if desired. Serve immediately.

Moroccan Chicken

SERVES 4-6

PRESSURE TIMING: 16 MINUTES, DIVIDED

A potpourri of exotic spices is featured in this signature dish of great Middle Eastern cuisine. This dish is a crowd-pleaser, so plan to make it for your next dinner party or other festive occasion.

2 TABLESPOONS OLIVE OIL

ONE 3½- TO 4-POUND CHICKEN, CUT INTO 8 PIECES

2 CUPS CHOPPED ONION

4 GARLIC CLOVES, MINCED

2 TEASPOONS GRATED FRESH GINGER

2 TEASPOONS DRIED CUMIN

2 TEASPOONS DRIED CORIANDER

2 TEASPOONS SALT

½ TEASPOON CAYENNE PEPPER

¼ CUP WATER

1 BUTTERNUT SQUASH (ABOUT 2 POUNDS), PEELED AND CUT INTO
    1-INCH CHUNKS

3 LARGE CARROTS, PEELED AND CUT INTO ½-INCH PIECES

ONE 15-OUNCE CAN CHICKPEAS, RINSED AND DRAINED

½ CUP RAISINS

1. In the bottom of the pressure cooker or in a skillet on the stove top, heat the oil over medium-high heat until it shines. Brown the chicken in batches, turning once, about 4 minutes. Remove the chicken to a plate.

2. Add to the oil the onion, garlic, ginger, cumin, coriander, salt, and cayenne. Cook for 1 minute. Combine the onion-spice mixture, water, chicken, squash, and carrots in the pressure cooker. Bring the pressure to high (15 psi) and cook for 15 minutes. Use the Quick Release method.

3. Stir in the chickpeas and raisins. Again bring the pressure to high (15 psi) and cook for 1 more minute. Use the Quick Release method. Serve immediately.

Spicy Chicken with Vermicelli

SERVES 4

PRESSURE TIMING: 8 MINUTES

In this recipe, boneless chicken cubes are cooked in the pressure cooker and the sauce is finished on the stove top. If you like the flavors of Thai food, you will love this dish.

1 POUND BONELESS, SKINLESS CHICKEN BREASTS, CUT INTO
   1-INCH CHUNKS

1 CUP REDUCED-SODIUM CHICKEN BROTH

4 GARLIC CLOVES, MINCED

10 OUNCES VERMICELLI

1 RED BELL PEPPER, SEEDED AND CUT INTO STRIPS

1½ CUPS THINLY SLICED SCALLIONS

1 TABLESPOON GRATED FRESH GINGER

½ TEASPOON RED PEPPER FLAKES

2 TABLESPOONS PEANUT BUTTER

1 TEASPOON REDUCED-SODIUM SOY SAUCE

3 TABLESPOONS UNSALTED CHOPPED PEANUTS

3 TABLESPOONS CHOPPED FRESH PARSLEY

1. Combine the chicken, broth, and garlic in the pressure cooker. Bring the pressure to high (15 psi) and cook for 8 minutes. Use the Natural Release method.

2. Meanwhile, bring a large pot of water to boil on the stove top. Cook the vermicelli until al dente according to the package instructions. Drain.

3. (Transfer the contents of the pressure cooker to a large pot on the stove top if necessary.) Add the bell pepper, scallions, ginger, and red pepper flakes and cook over medium-high heat until soft, 3 to 5 minutes.

4. In a small bowl, whisk together the peanut butter and soy sauce. Stir the mixture into the pot and continue cooking for 3 more minutes. Serve the chicken with the vermicelli and sprinkle the chopped peanuts and parsley over all.

Chicken Liver Pâté

SERVES 6-8

PRESSURE TIMING: 3 MINUTES

A delightfully inexpensive luxury, this easy-to-make pâté is marvelous slathered over toasted pieces of French bread. Serve as an appetizer at parties or with a large salad or bowl of soup for a complete meal.

2 TABLESPOONS VEGETABLE OIL

1 ONION, CHOPPED

1 BAY LEAF

¾ POUND CHICKEN LIVERS

SALT AND GROUND BLACK PEPPER

¼ CUP DRY RED WINE OR SHERRY

2 ANCHOVIES IN OIL

2 TABLESPOONS CAPERS

2 TABLESPOONS UNSALTED BUTTER, AT ROOM TEMPERATURE

1. In the bottom of the pressure cooker or in a large skillet on the stove top, heat the oil over medium-high heat. Add the onion and bay leaf and sauté until soft, 5 to 7 minutes. Add the chicken livers and season with salt and pepper. Sauté until the livers are seared and brown, about 2 minutes. Add the red wine and stir, scraping up any brown bits from the bottom.

2. (If using a skillet, transfer the ingredients to the pressure cooker at this point.) Bring the pressure to high (15 psi) and cook for 3 minutes. Use the Quick Release method.

3. Discard the bay leaf. Transfer the liver and cooking juices to a food processor. Add the anchovies, capers, and butter. Process until smooth and serve.

Lemon Chicken

SERVES 4–6

PRESSURE TIMING: 8 MINUTES

Here, chicken is paired with one of its favorite compatible flavors, lemon. Allow a few hours or up to overnight to marinate the chicken. Serve the lemon chicken with pasta, rice, or mashed potatoes.

ONE 3 ½- TO 4-POUND CHICKEN, CUT INTO 8 PIECES
¼ CUP PLUS 2 TABLESPOONS VEGETABLE OIL, DIVIDED
¼ CUP FRESH LEMON JUICE
1 TABLESPOON DRIED OREGANO
SALT AND GROUND BLACK PEPPER TO TASTE
½ CUP REDUCED-SODIUM CHICKEN BROTH

1. Put the chicken pieces in a large zip-top plastic bag. In a small bowl, whisk together ¼ cup of the oil, the lemon juice, oregano, salt, and pepper. Pour the marinade over the chicken pieces and toss to coat. Marinate in the refrigerator for at least 3 hours.

2. Remove the chicken pieces from the marinade (reserve the marinade). In the bottom of the pressure cooker or in a skillet on the stove top, heat the remaining 2 tablespoons oil over medium-high heat. When the oil shines, add the chicken pieces, in batches if necessary, and brown each side, about 4 minutes.

3. Combine the marinade, chicken, and broth in the pressure cooker; bring the pressure to high (15 psi) and cook for 8 minutes. Use the Quick Release method. Serve immediately.

Beer Can Chicken

SERVES 4

PRESSURE TIMING: 25 MINUTES

Yes, you can make this grilling classic in the pressure cooker. Those who love beer can chicken really love it made this way. Just make sure your cooker is tall enough for the bird to fit "standing up."

2 TABLESPOONS CHOPPED FRESH SAGE

2 TABLESPOONS CHOPPED FRESH THYME

1 TABLESPOON CHOPPED FRESH ROSEMARY

4 TABLESPOONS OLIVE OIL, DIVIDED

ZEST AND JUICE OF 1 LEMON

1 TEASPOON SALT

ONE 3½- TO 4-POUND CHICKEN

2 TABLESPOONS OLIVE OIL

ONE 12-OUNCE CAN BEER, DIVIDED

2 BAY LEAVES

1. In a small bowl, combine the sage, thyme, rosemary, 2 tablespoons of the oil, lemon juice, and salt. Rub the mixture all over the outside of the chicken and under the skin, where possible.

2. In the bottom of the pressure cooker or in a large skillet on the stove top, heat the remaining 2 tablespoons oil over medium-high heat. When it shines, brown the chicken on all sides.

3. Add one-third of the beer, half of the lemon zest, and 1 bay leaf to the cooker. Drop the remaining zest and bay leaf into the two-thirds-full can of beer. Stand the can in the middle of the pressure cooker and lower the bird onto the can.

4. Bring the pressure to high (15 psi) and cook for 25 minutes. Use the Natural Release method. Serve immediately.

Chicken Curry

SERVES 4–6

PRESSURE TIMING: 12 MINUTES

This recipe calls for the chicken to be finished on top of the stove after it has been pressure cooked.

2 TABLESPOONS OLIVE OIL

2 BONELESS, SKINLESS CHICKEN BREASTS, CUT INTO 1-INCH PIECES

2 ONIONS, CHOPPED

2 GARLIC CLOVES, MINCED

2 TABLESPOONS CURRY POWDER

1 APPLE, PEELED, CORED, AND DICED

SALT AND GROUND BLACK PEPPER

2 CUPS REDUCED-SODIUM CHICKEN BROTH

¾ CUP WATER

2 TABLESPOONS FLOUR

1 CUP PLAIN LOW-FAT GREEK YOGURT

4 CUPS COOKED RICE

1. In the bottom of the pressure cooker or in a skillet on the stove top, heat the oil over medium-high heat. When hot, add the chicken pieces, in batches if necessary, and brown on all sides. Transfer the chicken to a plate and set aside.

2. Add the onions and cook until golden, 4 to 6 minutes. Add the garlic and cook for another minute. Stir in the curry powder and diced apple. Season with salt and pepper.

3. Combine the onion-apple mixture, chicken, broth, and water in the pressure cooker and mix well. Bring the pressure to high (15 psi) and cook for 12 minutes. Use the Natural Release method.

4. In a small bowl, whisk together the flour and yogurt. Slowly stir the mixture into the pressure cooker. Transfer the contents of the cooker to a large pot if necessary and simmer over high heat for 3 minutes. Serve with the cooked rice.

Barbecue Chicken

SERVES 4-6

PRESSURE TIMING: 10 MINUTES

Grilling outside isn't always practical, so here is a taste of the great outdoors, fresh from the pressure cooker.

2 TABLESPOONS VEGETABLE OIL

ONE 3½- TO 4-POUND CHICKEN, CUT INTO 8 PIECES

2 CUPS BARBECUE SAUCE

2 ONIONS, CHOPPED

1 GREEN BELL PEPPER, SEEDED AND CHOPPED

1. In the bottom of the pressure cooker or in a skillet on the stove top, heat the oil over medium-high heat until it shines. Add the chicken pieces, in batches if necessary, and brown on all sides, about 4 minutes.

2. Combine the chicken, barbecue sauce, onions, and bell pepper in the pressure cooker; bring the pressure to medium (12 psi) and cook for 10 minutes. Use the Natural Release method. Serve immediately.

CHAPTER NINE

Pork

Spanish Pork

SERVES 6-8

PRESSURE TIMING: 40 MINUTES

This recipe takes a little longer than most others in this book, but the delectable morsels of pork will be worth the wait. Serve with Perfect Rice (page 54), which you can prepare quickly in your pressure cooker while the pork is resting after cooking.

3 TABLESPOONS OLIVE OIL

5 POUNDS PORK BUTT, CUT INTO ½-INCH CUBES

½ CUP MINCED ONION

6 GARLIC CLOVES, MINCED

1 TABLESPOON PAPRIKA

2 CUPS DRY RED WINE

2 CUPS REDUCED-SODIUM CHICKEN BROTH

½ CUP FRESH LEMON JUICE

¼ CUP CHOPPED FRESH PARSLEY

1. In the bottom of the pressure cooker or in a skillet on the stove top, heat the oil over medium-high heat until it shines. Brown the meat on all sides.

2. Combine the browned meat, onion, garlic, paprika, red wine, chicken broth, and lemon juice in the pressure cooker; bring the pressure to high (15 psi) and cook for 40 minutes. Use the Natural Release method. Transfer the pork to a serving dish, sprinkle the parsley over the top, and serve.

Pork Roast with Apples

SERVES 6

PRESSURE TIMING: 45 MINUTES

Pork and apples have an affinity for one another. This roast takes only 45 minutes to cook but is worthy of a special Sunday dinner. Serve over egg noodles.

1 TABLESPOON BROWN SUGAR

1 TEASPOON CARAWAY SEED, CRUSHED

½ TEASPOON SALT

ONE 3- TO 3½-POUND PORK SHOULDER ROAST, TRIMMED

2 TABLESPOONS VEGETABLE OIL

1 ONION, CUT INTO WEDGES

1 CUP WATER

½ CUP APPLE JUICE

¼ CUP APPLE CIDER

3 APPLES, CORED AND CUT INTO WEDGES

1. In a small bowl, combine the brown sugar, caraway, and salt. Rub the mixture all over the outside of the pork. In the bottom of the pressure cooker or in a large skillet on the stove top, heat the oil over medium-high heat and brown the meat on all sides.

2. Combine the pork, onion, water, juice, and cider in the pressure cooker; bring the pressure to high (15 psi) and cook for 45 minutes. Use the Natural Release method.

3. Remove the roast to a platter and tent with aluminum foil. Add the apple wedges to the juices from the roast (transfer the contents to a medium saucepan if necessary) and simmer on the stove top over high heat for 3 minutes. Remove the foil, pour the apples and juices over the roast, and serve immediately.

Pork Tenderloin

You'll find many recipes for pork tenderloin, but this one—not overly fussy, yet maximizing the blend of flavors—is a surefire winner every time.

¼ CUP OLIVE OIL

¼ CUP FRESH LIME JUICE

¼ CUP CHOPPED FRESH CILANTRO

3 GARLIC CLOVES, MINCED

½ TEASPOON RED PEPPER FLAKES, OR TO TASTE

½ TEASPOON SALT, OR TO TASTE

ONE 1-POUND PORK TENDERLOIN

2 TABLESPOONS VEGETABLE OIL

¾ CUP REDUCED-SODIUM CHICKEN BROTH

¼ CUP FRESH LEMON JUICE

1. Combine the olive oil, lime juice, cilantro, garlic, red pepper flakes, and salt in a large zip-top plastic bag. Add the tenderloin and turn to coat. Marinate in the refrigerator for at least 6 hours or overnight.

2. Remove the tenderloin from the marinade (reserve the marinade) and pat dry. In the bottom of the pressure cooker or in a skillet on the stove top, heat the vegetable oil over medium-high heat until it shines. Add the tenderloin and brown on all sides.

3. Combine the marinade, tenderloin, chicken broth, and lemon juice in the pressure cooker; bring the pressure to high (15 psi) and cook for 25 minutes. Use the Natural Release method.

4. Transfer the meat to a cutting board and let rest 5 minutes. Slice into medallions, arrange on a platter, and pour any cooking liquid over the meat. Serve immediately.

Baby Back Ribs

SERVES 6

PRESSURE TIMING: 20 MINUTES

These ribs are the perfect solution for when the snow is too deep to find the grill.

3 POUNDS BABY BACK RIBS

ONE 18-OUNCE BOTTLE BARBECUE SAUCE

½ CUP WATER

1. Cut the ribs into small sections. Place the ribs in a large bowl and cover with the barbecue sauce. Let sit at room temperature for 30 minutes.

2. Lean the rib sections against the inside walls of the pressure cooker. Pour the water and 1 cup of the barbecue sauce into the cooker (discard the remaining sauce). Bring the pressure to high (15 psi) and cook for 20 minutes. Use the Natural Release method. Serve immediately.

Pork Chops with Potatoes

SERVES 8

PRESSURE TIMING: 15 MINUTES

Rich, meaty chops accompanied by savory vegetables will get everyone to the dinner table on time.

SALT

8 CENTER-CUT PORK CHOPS

½ CUP UNSALTED BUTTER, DIVIDED

6 MEDIUM POTATOES

1 CUP WATER

1 TABLESPOON WORCESTERSHIRE SAUCE

1 ONION, THINLY SLICED

3 POUNDS CARROTS, SCRUBBED AND CUT INTO CHUNKS

1. Salt both sides of the pork chops. In a large skillet, heat ¼ cup of the butter over medium-high heat. Brown the chops, in batches if necessary, for 2 minutes on each side. Set the chops aside.

2. Melt the remaining ¼ cup butter in the skillet, add the potatoes, and cook, stirring, for 3 minutes.

3. Pour the water and the Worcestershire sauce into the pressure cooker. Add the potatoes. Lay the chops over the potatoes, put the onions on the chops, and place the carrots on top. Bring the pressure to high (15 psi) and cook for 15 minutes. Use the Quick Release method.

4. Arrange the chops on a platter. Spoon the vegetables around the meat and pour any cooking liquid over all. Serve immediately.

Pork Vindaloo

SERVES 4

PRESSURE TIMING: 15 MINUTES

This is a spicy classic from India that takes no time at all to make using a pressure cooker. Serve with warm basmati rice or crusty rolls.

2 TABLESPOONS UNSALTED BUTTER

1 TABLESPOON CANOLA OIL

1 ONION, CHOPPED

1 POUND BONELESS PORK, CUT INTO 1-INCH CUBES

2 TEASPOONS WHOLE CUMIN SEEDS

½ CUP WATER

¼ CUP REDUCED-SODIUM CHICKEN BROTH

ONE 14-OUNCE CAN COCONUT MILK

2 TABLESPOONS COARSE-GRAIN MUSTARD

1 TEASPOON GROUND TURMERIC

½ TEASPOON SALT

½ TEASPOON CAYENNE PEPPER

TWO 10-OUNCE PACKAGES FROZEN CHOPPED SPINACH

2 POUNDS YUKON GOLD POTATOES, SCRUBBED AND CUT INTO
    2-INCH PIECES

1. In the bottom of the pressure cooker or in a large skillet on the stove top, melt the butter in the oil over medium-high heat. Add the onion and sauté until golden, 3 to 5 minutes. Add the pork cubes and cumin seeds and sauté until the meat begins to brown, about 5 minutes. Add the water and simmer, scraping up any browned bits, for about 3 minutes.

2. Combine the meat and cooking liquid with the broth, coconut milk, mustard, turmeric, salt, and cayenne in the pressure cooker. Break off cubes of frozen spinach and add them to the cooker. Top with the potatoes. Bring the pressure to high (15 psi) and cook for 15 minutes. Use the Natural Release method. Transfer the contents of the cooker to a large bowl and serve immediately.

Sweet and Sour Pork Ribs

SERVES 4
PRESSURE TIMING: 30 MINUTES

Ever popular for its inviting appearance and great blend of flavors, this easy recipe is great to serve at home or take to an outdoor party. Make small ribs for appetizers or larger ribs for a main course.

3 POUNDS SPARE RIBS
2 TABLESPOONS VEGETABLE OIL
¼ CUP KETCHUP
3 TABLESPOONS MINCED ONION
3 TABLESPOONS APRICOT MARMALADE
3 TABLESPOONS CIDER VINEGAR
2 TABLESPOONS DRY SHERRY
1 TEASPOON HOT PEPPER SAUCE, OR TO TASTE

1. Cut the ribs into small sections. In the bottom of the pressure cooker or in a large skillet on the stove top, heat the oil over medium-high heat. Add the ribs, in batches if necessary, and brown on all sides. Remove to a plate.

2. In a medium bowl, combine the ketchup, onion, marmalade, vinegar, sherry, and hot pepper sauce and stir until completely mixed. Pour the sauce into the pressure cooker.

3. Add the ribs to the sauce; bring the pressure to high (15 psi) and cook for 30 minutes. Use the Natural Release method. Place the ribs on a platter, pour any sauce left in the cooker into a bowl, and serve.

Black Currant–Glazed Pork Chops

SERVES 4

PRESSURE TIMING: 1 MINUTE

These chops are glazed with black currant jelly and literally cook in 1 minute. The flavorful sauce makes these chops perfect to serve with rice.

2 TABLESPOONS VEGETABLE OIL

4 PORK LOIN CHOPS, ABOUT 1 INCH THICK

SALT AND GROUND BLACK PEPPER

⅓ CUP WHITE WINE VINEGAR

½ CUP BLACK CURRANT JELLY

3 TABLESPOONS BROWN SUGAR

2 TABLESPOONS DIJON MUSTARD

1. In a large skillet, heat the oil over medium-high heat until shiny. Season the chops with salt and pepper and brown them, about 3 minutes per side. Remove and set aside.

2. Pour the white wine vinegar into the skillet and simmer, scraping up any browned bits from the bottom and sides. Pour the liquid into the pressure cooker.

3. In a small bowl, whisk together the jelly, brown sugar, and mustard. Slather the mixture on both sides of the pork chops. Place the rack in the pressure cooker and set the chops on the rack. Bring the pressure to high (15 psi) and cook for 1 minute. Use the Natural Release method.

4. Set the chops on a platter and tent with aluminum foil to keep warm. Boil the sauce left in the bottom of the cooker until thick and syrupy, 2 to 3 minutes. Pour the syrup over the meat and serve immediately.

Rustic Pork and Hominy Stew

SERVES 4

PRESSURE TIMING: 13 MINUTES

Hearty and warm, this stew is delectable served with crusty bread and butter.

SALT

1¼ POUNDS PORK SHOULDER, CUT INTO 1-INCH CUBES

2 TABLESPOONS OLIVE OIL

1 ONION, CHOPPED

4 GARLIC CLOVES, MINCED

1 TEASPOON MINCED CHIPOTLE IN ADOBO SAUCE

1 TEASPOON DRIED OREGANO

½ TEASPOON GROUND CUMIN

2 CUPS REDUCED-SODIUM CHICKEN BROTH, DIVIDED

ONE 29-OUNCE CAN HOMINY, RINSED AND DRAINED

ONE 14.5-OUNCE CAN DICED TOMATOES, DRAINED

¼ CUP CHOPPED FRESH CILANTRO

¼ CUP SLICED JALAPEÑO PEPPERS

1. Salt the pork cubes. In the bottom of the pressure cooker or in a large skillet, heat the oil over medium-high heat until it shines. Add the meat and brown on all sides, 4 to 6 minutes. Remove to a plate.

2. Combine the meat, onion, garlic, chipotle in adobo, oregano, cumin, and broth in the pressure cooker. Bring the pressure to medium (12 psi) and cook for 13 minutes. Use the Natural Release method.

3. (Transfer the contents of the pressure cooker to a large pot if necessary). Stir in the hominy and tomatoes and simmer over medium heat, uncovered, for 20 minutes. Serve in bowls, garnishing with the cilantro and jalapeños.

CHAPTER TEN

Beef and Lamb

Yankee Pot Roast

SERVES 6-8

PRESSURE TIMING: 39 MINUTES, DIVIDED

Yankee pot roast is perhaps the reason to begin using a pressure cooker. This winter culinary classic is ready in about 40 minutes with a pressure cooker. Feel free to add other root vegetables, such rutabagas and sweet potatoes, and serve with hot egg noodles.

ONE 3- TO 4-POUND BEEF CHUCK OR ROUND ROAST

4 GARLIC CLOVES, SLIVERED

½ CUP FLOUR

1 TEASPOON SALT

1 TEASPOON GROUND BLACK PEPPER

3 TABLESPOONS VEGETABLE OIL

1 CUP CHOPPED ONION

½ CUP DRY RED WINE

3 CUPS REDUCED-SODIUM BEEF BROTH

ONE 28-OUNCE CAN DICED TOMATOES, DRAINED

1 TEASPOON DRIED THYME

1 TEASPOON CHOPPED FRESH ROSEMARY

6 MEDIUM RED POTATOES, SCRUBBED AND QUARTERED

4 CARROTS, SCRUBBED AND CUT INTO ½-INCH PIECES

4 CELERY STALKS, THINLY SLICED

1 CUP THINLY SLICED PARSNIPS

¼ CUP CHOPPED FRESH PARSLEY

1. With a sharp paring knife, make small cuts all over the meat, about 1 inch deep, and tuck garlic slivers deep into the roast. In a small bowl, combine the flour, salt, and pepper. Rub the seasoned flour all over the meat.

2. In the bottom of the pressure cooker or in a large skillet on the stove top, heat the oil over medium-high heat. As soon as the oil shines, brown the meat on all sides.

3. Add the onion and cook alongside the meat until softened. Add the wine and simmer for 2 to 3 minutes, scraping up any browned bits.

4. Combine the meat, onion and wine mixture with the broth, tomatoes, thyme, and rosemary in the pressure cooker. Bring the pressure to high (15 psi) and cook for 35 minutes. Use the Natural Release method.

5. Add the potatoes, carrots, celery, and parsnips. Bring the pressure to high (15 psi) and cook for 4 more minutes. Use the Quick Release method. Stir in the parsley and serve.

Southern-Style Beef Ribs

SERVES 6

PRESSURE TIMING: 30 MINUTES

What makes this dish Southern? The Coca-Cola, of course. Do not use diet cola!
Serve these ribs on a mound of mashed potatoes with the thick juices spooned
on top.

2 TEASPOONS PAPRIKA

2 TEASPOONS GROUND BLACK PEPPER

2 TEASPOONS CAYENNE PEPPER

1 TEASPOON GROUND CUMIN

1 TEASPOON SALT

4 TO 5 POUNDS ENGLISH-CUT BEEF SHORT RIBS, CUT CROSSWISE INTO
  2½-INCH-LONG PIECES

3 TABLESPOONS OLIVE OIL

6 GARLIC CLOVES, PEELED AND SMASHED

1 MEDIUM ONION, DICED

2 CUPS COCA-COLA (NOT DIET)

2 TABLESPOONS REDUCED-SODIUM SOY SAUCE

2 TABLESPOONS WORCESTERSHIRE SAUCE

2 TABLESPOONS CORNSTARCH

3 TABLESPOONS WATER

HOT MASHED POTATOES, FOR SERVING

1. In a small bowl, combine the paprika, black pepper, cayenne pepper, cumin, and salt and rub the mixture all over the ribs.

2. In the bottom of the pressure cooker or in a large skillet on the stove top, heat the oil over medium-high heat until it shines. Add the beef ribs, in batches if necessary, and brown on all sides. Remove to a plate.

3. Add the garlic, onion, cola, soy sauce, and Worcestershire sauce and simmer, scraping up the browned bits, for 2 to 3 minutes.

4. (If using a skillet, transfer the ingredients to the pressure cooker at this point.) Add the browned ribs, turning the meat to coat. Bring the pressure to medium (12 psi) and cook for 30 minutes. Use the Natural Release method.

5. Remove the ribs to a platter and tent with aluminum foil to keep warm. Pour the juices from the pressure cooker through a fine-mesh sieve to strain out the onion and garlic. Return the strained juices to the pressure cooker or to a small saucepan on the stove top over medium-low heat. In a small bowl, whisk the cornstarch into the water. Add the mixture to the hot juices, stirring constantly, until thickened.

6. Mound mashed potatoes on each plate, put a couple of ribs on top, and spoon the thickened gravy over all. Serve.

Beef Stroganoff

SERVES 6

PRESSURE TIMING: 20 MINUTES

This dish came out of nineteenth-century Russia and has been loved worldwide in its many variations ever since. Substitute yogurt for the sour cream if you prefer. If you like mushrooms, add them.

¾ CUP FLOUR

1 TEASPOON SALT

1 TEASPOON GROUND BLACK PEPPER

1 TEASPOON ONION POWDER

1 TEASPOON DRIED THYME

1 TEASPOON DRIED ROSEMARY

½ TEASPOON PAPRIKA

ONE 3½-POUND SIRLOIN TIP ROAST, CUT INTO CUBES

3 TABLESPOONS OLIVE OIL

1 ONION, THINLY SLICED

4 GARLIC CLOVES, MINCED

1¾ CUPS REDUCED-SODIUM BEEF BROTH

¼ CUP DRY RED WINE

1 CUP SOUR CREAM

HOT EGG NOODLES, FOR SERVING

1. In a large bowl, combine the flour, salt, pepper, onion powder, thyme, rosemary, and paprika. Toss the meat cubes in the seasoned flour. In the bottom of the pressure cooker or in a large skillet on the stove top, heat the oil over medium-high heat. When the oil is shiny, brown the meat, in batches if necessary.

2. Combine the browned meat, onion, garlic, broth, and red wine in the pressure cooker; bring the pressure to high (15 psi) and cook for 20 minutes. Use the Natural Release method.

3. Put half of the sour cream in a medium bowl and stir in a heaping spoonful of the hot liquid from the pressure cooker. Add the rest of the sour cream to the bowl and continue to mix in spoonfuls of hot liquid. When all of the hot liquid has been mixed into the sour cream, pour the mixture back into the pressure cooker and stir well. Spoon the stroganoff over the hot egg noodles and serve.

All-American Chili

SERVES 6-8

PRESSURE TIMING: 8 MINUTES

Ground beef is the main ingredient in this hearty chili—8 minutes, and dinner's on the table. Serve with biscuits or cornbread, and include bowls of shredded Cheddar cheese, chopped fresh cilantro, and sour cream to add to the chili.

2 TABLESPOONS OLIVE OIL

1 POUND LEAN GROUND BEEF

1 ONION, CHOPPED

1 GREEN BELL PEPPER, SEEDED AND CHOPPED

1 JALAPEÑO PEPPER, SEEDED AND CHOPPED

3 GARLIC CLOVES, MINCED

ONE 28-OUNCE CAN DICED TOMATOES, DRAINED

3 TABLESPOONS TOMATO PASTE

1 TABLESPOON BROWN SUGAR

2 TEASPOONS UNSWEETENED COCOA POWDER

2 TABLESPOONS CHILI POWDER

2 TEASPOONS GROUND CUMIN

1 TEASPOON SALT, OR TO TASTE

½ TEASPOON RED PEPPER FLAKES, OR TO TASTE

1 CUP REDUCED-SODIUM BEEF BROTH

½ CUP WATER

TWO 15-OUNCE CANS DARK RED KIDNEY BEANS, RINSED AND DRAINED

1. In the bottom of the pressure cooker or in a large skillet on the stove top, heat the oil over medium-high heat and brown the meat. Add the onion, bell and jalapeño peppers, and garlic to the meat and continue to cook until the onion softens, 2 to 3 minutes.

2. Combine in the pressure cooker the meat mixture, tomatoes, tomato paste, brown sugar, cocoa powder, chili powder, cumin, salt, red pepper flakes, broth, and water. Bring the pressure to high (15 psi) and cook for 8 minutes. Use the Natural Release method. Stir in the drained beans (transfer the contents of the pressure cooker to a large stockpot if necessary) and heat through on the stove top over medium heat. Serve.

Beef Curry

SERVES 6

PRESSURE TIMING: 24 MINUTES, DIVIDED

Curry is a beloved dish because of its flavor and endless variations. Add grated coconut, different types of curry powder, lime zest, chopped nuts, chopped vegetables, fresh herbs . . . whatever appeals to you. Serve over basmati rice.

2 TABLESPOONS VEGETABLE OIL

3 POUNDS BEEF CHUCK, CUT INTO 2-INCH CUBES

2 ONIONS, HALVED AND CUT INTO ½-INCH-THICK SLICES

ONE 14-OUNCE CAN COCONUT MILK

ONE 4-OUNCE JAR CURRY PASTE

1 CUP REDUCED-SODIUM CHICKEN BROTH OR WATER

1 TABLESPOON FISH SAUCE

1 TABLESPOON REDUCED-SODIUM SOY SAUCE

2 TABLESPOONS BROWN SUGAR

1 TEASPOON SALT

1½ POUNDS NEW POTATOES, SCRUBBED

1. In the bottom of the pressure cooker or in a large skillet on the stove top, heat the oil over medium-high heat until it shines. Add the meat, in batches if necessary, and brown on all sides, about 6 minutes. Add the onions and cook until softened, 3 to 4 minutes.

2. Combine the meat, onions, coconut milk, curry paste, broth, fish sauce, soy sauce, brown sugar, and salt in the pressure cooker. Bring the pressure to high (15 psi) and cook for 20 minutes. Use the Natural Release method.

3. Stir the potatoes into the curry. Bring the pressure to high (15 psi) and cook for 4 more minutes. Use the Quick Release Method. Serve immediately.

Meatballs

SERVES 6-8

PRESSURE TIMING: 10 MINUTES

All that's needed to make a great meatball is confidence. If you have a pressure cooker, it's confidence plus 10 minutes. Serve over spaghetti with tomato sauce and a sprinkling of grated Parmesan or Romano cheese, or in crusty rolls with melted Provolone for hearty sandwiches.

1½ POUNDS LEAN GROUND BEEF

2 EGGS, BEATEN UNTIL FROTHY

½ CUP LONG-GRAIN WHITE RICE

1 SMALL ONION, MINCED

¼ CUP CHOPPED FRESH PARSLEY

1 TEASPOON SALT

¼ TEASPOON GROUND BLACK PEPPER

3 TABLESPOONS OLIVE OIL

1 TABLESPOON DRIED OREGANO

1 CUP TOMATO JUICE

½ CUP WATER

¼ CUP TOMATO PASTE

1. Place the ground beef in a large bowl. Add the beaten eggs, rice, onion, parsley, salt, and pepper and mix with your clean hands until fully combined. Form the mixture into meatballs about 1½ inches in diameter.

2. In the bottom of the pressure cooker or in a large skillet on the stove top, heat the oil over medium-high heat. When the oil shines, add the meatballs, in batches if necessary, and brown on all sides, 3 to 4 minutes.

3. Combine the browned meatballs, oregano, tomato juice, water, and tomato paste in the pressure cooker; bring the pressure to high (15 psi) and cook for 10 minutes. Use the Natural Release method. Serve immediately.

Moroccan Beef or Lamb

SERVES 6

PRESSURE TIMING: 45 MINUTES

A Middle Eastern staple, preserved lemons are made by splitting the fruits open and packing them in a mixture of salt and lemon juice. The flavor has a distinctive, delicious bite and powerful acidic properties that tenderize tough meat. Preserved lemons are available in many grocery stores and can be ordered online. Serve this dish over basmati rice.

1 TABLESPOON UNSALTED BUTTER

⅓ CUP OLIVE OIL

1½ POUNDS BEEF CHUCK OR LAMB SHOULDER, CUT INTO 2-INCH PIECES

1 LARGE ONION, MINCED

3 GARLIC CLOVES, MINCED

½ TEASPOON SALT

½ TEASPOON GROUND BLACK PEPPER

½ TEASPOON GROUND GINGER

½ TEASPOON GROUND TURMERIC

¼ CUP CHOPPED FRESH PARSLEY AND/OR CILANTRO

½ TEASPOON SAFFRON THREADS, CRUMBLED

2½ TO 3 CUPS WATER

½ CUP RED OR GREEN OLIVES, WITH PITS

1 PRESERVED LEMON, QUARTERED AND SEEDED

1. In the bottom of the pressure cooker or in a large skillet on the stove top, melt the butter in the oil over medium-high heat. When the oil is shiny and hot, add the meat, in batches if necessary, and brown on all sides, 6 to 8 minutes. Add the onion, garlic, salt, pepper, ginger, and turmeric and continue to cook, stirring, for 1 minute.

2. (If using a skillet, transfer the ingredients to the pressure cooker at this point.) Add the parsley and/or cilantro, saffron, and water; bring the pressure to high (15 psi) and cook for 45 minutes. Use the Natural Release method. Stir in the preserved lemon and serve.

Lamb Shanks with Gravy

SERVES 6

PRESSURE TIMING: 25 MINUTES

Here you go, lamb lovers. Serving these shanks atop mashed potatoes allows you to catch every drop of the delicious homemade gravy.

¼ CUP PLUS 2 TABLESPOONS FLOUR, DIVIDED

SALT AND GROUND BLACK PEPPER

6 LAMB SHANKS, PREFERABLY FRENCHED

3 TABLESPOONS OLIVE OIL

1 ONION, CHOPPED

3 GARLIC CLOVES, MINCED

½ CUP DRY RED WINE

3 CARROTS, PEELED AND CUT INTO 1-INCH PIECES

½ CUP FRESH OR CANNED DICED TOMATOES

¼ CUP REDUCED-SODIUM BEEF BROTH

1 TEASPOON DRIED OREGANO

1 TEASPOON LEMON ZEST

¼ CUP COLD WATER

HOT MASHED POTATOES, FOR SERVING

1. In a medium bowl, generously season ¼ cup of the flour with salt and pepper. Roll the shanks in the seasoned flour mix.

2. In the bottom of the pressure cooker or in a large skillet on the stove top, heat the oil over medium-high heat. When the oil is hot and shiny, brown the shanks on all sides, in batches if necessary, and set aside on a plate.

3. Add the onion and garlic and sauté until soft, about 4 minutes. Add the wine and simmer for 3 minutes longer, scraping up any browned bits.

4. Combine the meat, wine and onion mixture, carrots, tomatoes, beef broth, oregano, and lemon zest in the pressure cooker. Bring the pressure to high (15 psi) and cook for 25 minutes. Use the Natural Release method.

5. Remove the shanks to a platter and tent with aluminum foil to keep warm.

6. Make the gravy by heating the meat juices on the stove top over high heat (transfer the juices to a small saucepan if necessary). In a small bowl, whisk the remaining 2 tablespoons flour into the cold water until smooth. Slowly stir the flour mixture into the hot pan juices and stir constantly until thickened.

7. Pile mashed potatoes on each plate, top with a shank, and pour the gravy over all. Serve immediately.

Leg of Lamb

SERVES 6

PRESSURE TIMING: 25 MINUTES

*The large cubes of lamb cook to tender perfection in this recipe. Serve with
basmati rice, chopped fresh cilantro, and sweet chutney.*

3 TABLESPOON VEGETABLE OIL

ONE 4- TO 5-POUND BONELESS LEG OF LAMB, CUT INTO 3-INCH CUBES

1 LARGE ONION, CHOPPED

6 GARLIC CLOVES, MINCED

1 CUP DRY RED WINE

2 LARGE CARROTS, SCRUBBED AND CHOPPED

¼ CUP PRUNES

¼ CUP DRIED APRICOTS

1 TABLESPOON DRIED THYME

1 TABLESPOON LEMON ZEST

1½ CUPS REDUCED-SODIUM BEEF BROTH

2 TABLESPOON REDUCED-SODIUM SOY SAUCE

1. In the bottom of the pressure cooker or in a large skillet on the stove top,
heat the oil over medium-high heat. When the oil is hot and shiny, add the
lamb cubes, in batches if necessary, and brown on all sides, 6 to 8 minutes.
Add the onion and garlic and continue to cook until the onion has softened,
about 3 minutes. Add the wine and simmer for 3 minutes more.

2. Combine the meat and onion mixture with the carrots, prunes, apricots,
thyme, lemon zest, broth, and soy sauce in the pressure cooker. Bring the
pressure to high (15 psi) and cook for 25 minutes. Use the Natural Release
method. Serve immediately.

Lamb Curry

The heat in this dish is up to you, depending on the curry powder you use. Serve with hot basmati rice.

3 TABLESPOONS VEGETABLE OIL

2 POUNDS BONELESS LAMB LEG OR SHOULDER, CUT INTO 1-INCH CHUNKS

3 ONIONS, CHOPPED

6 GARLIC CLOVES, MINCED

1 TABLESPOON GRATED FRESH GINGER

2 TABLESPOONS CURRY POWDER, OR MORE TO TASTE

1 CUP WATER

1 LARGE POTATO, CUBED

1. In the bottom of the pressure cooker or in a large skillet on the stove top, heat the oil over medium-high heat. When the oil is hot and shiny, add the meat, in batches if necessary, and brown on all sides, 4 to 6 minutes. Add the onions, garlic, ginger, and curry powder and cook, stirring, until the onions are soft, about 4 minutes.

2. Combine the meat mixture, water, and potato in the pressure cooker; bring the pressure to high (15 psi) and cook for 8 minutes. Use the Natural Release method. Serve immediately.

Lamb Chops

SERVES 4

PRESSURE TIMING: 8 MINUTES

A thick lamb chop isn't always easy to prepare properly, but it will positively sing under this preparation. Serve alongside a baked potato or long-grain rice.

4 THICK-CUT LAMB CHOPS, UP TO 1 INCH

SALT AND GROUND BLACK PEPPER

3 TABLESPOONS VEGETABLE OIL

1½ CUPS CHOPPED ONION

2 GARLIC CLOVES, MINCED

¼ CUP DRY WHITE WINE

1½ CUPS CHOPPED CARROT

1 CUP REDUCED-SODIUM CHICKEN BROTH

1. Season both sides of the lamb chops with salt and pepper. In the bottom of the pressure cooker or in a large skillet on the stove top, heat the oil over medium-high heat. Brown the chops, about 2 minutes per side.

2. Remove the chops to a plate. Add the onion and garlic and cook until the onion is soft, about 3 minutes. Add the wine and simmer, scraping up any browned bits, for 2 to 3 minutes.

3. Combine the chops, onion mixture, carrot, and broth in the pressure cooker. Bring the pressure to high (15 psi) and cook for 8 minutes. Use the Quick Release method. Serve.

Lamb and Pea Stew

SERVES 4

PRESSURE TIMING: 12 MINUTES

For the best result, use balsamic vinegar in this stew. Serve with warm, crusty bread and a fruity extra-virgin olive oil for dipping.

2 POUNDS LAMB SHOULDER, CUT INTO 2-INCH CUBES

SALT AND GROUND BLACK PEPPER TO TASTE

2 TABLESPOONS OLIVE OIL

2 ONIONS, THINLY SLICED

6 GARLIC CLOVES, MINCED

¼ CUP BALSAMIC OR RED WINE VINEGAR

1 LARGE RED BELL PEPPER, SEEDED AND CUT INTO THIN STRIPS

1 LARGE GREEN BELL PEPPER, SEEDED AND CUT INTO THIN STRIPS

ONE 14.5-OUNCE CAN DICED TOMATOES, DRAINED

2 TABLESPOONS TOMATO PASTE

1 TEASPOON DRIED BASIL

1 TEASPOON DRIED OREGANO

⅓ CUP MINCED FRESH PARSLEY

ONE 10-OUNCE PACKAGE FROZEN GREEN PEAS, BROKEN APART

1. Season the lamb with salt and pepper on all sides. In the bottom of the pressure cooker or in a large skillet on the stove top, heat the oil over medium-high heat brown the meat on all sides, in batches if necessary. Remove to a plate.

2. Add the onions and garlic and sauté until the onion is soft, 3 to 4 minutes. Add the vinegar and simmer, scraping up any browned bits from the sides and bottom of the pan.

3. Combine the meat, onion mixture, bell peppers, tomatoes, tomato paste, basil, oregano, and parsley in the pressure cooker. Bring the pressure to high (15 psi) and cook for 12 minutes. Use the Quick Release method.

4. Open the lid, put the chunks of frozen peas atop the stew, and cover again but do not seal. Let the residual heat in the cooker steam the peas for 3 to 5 minutes. Stir and serve.

CHAPTER ELEVEN

Desserts

Fudge Drops

SERVES 6–8

PRESSURE TIMING: 5 MINUTES

If you have kids, this simple, sweet treat made in the cooker will keep them happy.

ONE 14-OUNCE CAN SWEETENED CONDENSED MILK

ONE 12-OUNCE BAG SEMISWEET CHOCOLATE CHIPS

2 CUPS WATER

1 CUP CHOPPED WALNUTS

1 TEASPOON PURE VANILLA EXTRACT

1. Combine the condensed milk and chocolate chips in a metal bowl that fits loosely in the pressure cooker. Cover the bowl with aluminum foil.

2. Pour the water into the bottom of the pressure cooker and place the bowl on the rack in the cooker. Bring the pressure to high (15 psi) and cook 5 minutes. Use the Quick Release method.

3. Fold the nuts and vanilla into the chocolate mixture and gently stir until smooth. Drop by teaspoonfuls into paper or foil candy cups, or onto waxed paper in the shape of candy kisses. Cool before serving.

Banana Pudding

SERVES 4

PRESSURE TIMING: 12 MINUTES

You'll need four 6-ounce ramekins or glass bowls for this delightful pudding. Serve with vanilla wafers if you really want to be a dessert star.

2 RIPE BANANAS

2 EGG YOLKS

1 EGG

¼ CUP SUGAR

½ CUP HALF-AND-HALF

¼ CUP SWEETENED CONDENSED MILK

¼ CUP SOUR CREAM

1 TEASPOON DARK RUM (OPTIONAL)

1 TEASPOON PURE VANILLA EXTRACT

2 CUPS WATER

1. Purée the bananas in a food processor or blender. Beat the egg yolks with the egg and add to the bananas. Pulse to mix. Add the sugar, half-and-half, condensed milk, sour cream, rum (if using), and vanilla. Pulse again until smooth. Fill the ramekins or bowls with the banana pudding.

2. Pour the water into the bottom of the pressure cooker. Place the ramekins or bowls on the rack in the pressure cooker. Bring the pressure to high (15 psi) and cook for 12 minutes. Use the Quick Release method. Serve immediately or transfer to the refrigerator and serve chilled.

Poached Pears

Simple and elegant, these pears are perfect for entertaining. With a total cook time of 7 minutes, you can step into the kitchen and truly "whip up" dessert for your guests.

4 LARGE, FIRM PEARS

ONE 750-MILLILITER BOTTLE FRUITY RED WINE

1¼ CUPS SUGAR, DIVIDED

1 CINNAMON STICK

1 TABLESPOON GROUND CLOVES

ZEST AND JUICE OF 1 ORANGE

½ CUP MASCARPONE CHEESE

1. Peel the pears. Slice a little bit off the wide bottom of each pear so that it can sit up straight on the dessert plate.

2. Combine the pears, wine, 1 cup of the sugar, cinnamon stick, cloves, and orange zest and juice in the pressure cooker. Bring the pressure to high (15 psi) and cook for 3 minutes. Use the Quick Release method.

3. In the meantime, in a small bowl, whisk the remaining ¼ cup sugar into the mascarpone.

4. After releasing the pressure, set a pear on each dessert plate. Boil the remaining liquid in the pressure cooker or in a small saucepan over high heat until thick and syrupy, 3 to 4 minutes. Spoon the sauce over the pears. Top with a dollop of the sweetened cheese and serve.

Rice Pudding with Raisins and Walnuts

SERVES 4

PRESSURE TIMING: 10 MINUTES

Anyone who pressure cooks should keep handy a recipe for rice pudding. This is a particularly easy and delicious version.

1½ CUPS ARBORIO RICE

¾ CUP SUGAR

1 TEASPOON SALT

5 CUPS LOW-FAT MILK

2 EGGS

1 CUP HALF-AND-HALF

2 TEASPOONS PURE VANILLA EXTRACT

1 CUP RAISINS

½ CUP WALNUT PIECES

1 TEASPOON GROUND CINNAMON

1. In the bottom of the pressure cooker or in a medium saucepan on the stove top, combine the rice, sugar, salt, and low-fat milk. Warm the mixture over medium heat, stirring until the sugar is dissolved. (If using a saucepan, transfer the ingredients to the pressure cooker at this point.) Bring the pressure to high (15 psi) and cook for 10 minutes. Use the Quick Release method.

2. In the meantime, in a medium bowl, whisk together the eggs, half-and-half, and vanilla.

3. After releasing the pressure, set the pressure cooker on the stove top over high heat (or return the mixture to the saucepan if necessary). Add the egg mixture and stir constantly until all of the ingredients are integrated, thick, and hot. Stir in the raisins and walnuts. Spoon into bowls, sprinkle some cinnamon atop each, and serve immediately.

Dulce de Leche

MAKES ABOUT 1 CUP

COOKING TIME: 20 MINUTES

Make this caramel-flavored dessert cream by simply cooking sweetened condensed milk and letting it cool. Pour on ice cream, spread on toasted bread, or use as a sweet dip for bananas. Store any leftovers in a covered container in the refrigerator for up to 1 week.

ONE 14-OUNCE CAN SWEETENED CONDENSED MILK, UNOPENED

WATER

1. Place the rack in the bottom of the pressure cooker and set the steamer basket on the rack. Remove the paper label (if any) from the can of milk. Lay the can of milk on its side in the steamer basket, making sure the edges of the can do not touch the sides of the pressure cooker. Pour in enough water to completely submerge the can, without going past the two-thirds mark on the pressure cooker. Bring the pressure to high (15 psi) and cook for 20 minutes. Use the Natural Release method.

2. Leave the can of milk sitting in the water in the pressure cooker overnight. The can must be fully cooled before you open it or the contents will still be under pressure. Open the cooled can and use the dulce de leche as desired.

Dulce de Leche Ice Cream Pie

SERVES 8

COOKING TIME: 20 MINUTES

Make the Dulce de Leche at least one day before you assemble this pie. You can use any flavor of ice cream.

ONE 16-OUNCE BOX CHOCOLATE WAFERS

¼ CUP UNSALTED BUTTER, MELTED, OR MORE IF NECESSARY

2 PINTS VANILLA ICE CREAM

FOUR 1.4-OUNCE CHOCOLATE-COVERED TOFFEE BARS, SUCH AS
    HEATH, CHOPPED

1 CAN DULCE DE LECHE (PAGE 134)

1. Preheat the oven to 350°F.

2. Process the chocolate wafers in a food processor, pouring the melted butter into the feed tube while the machine is running. If the cookies seem too dry to form a piecrust, add more melted butter by the tablespoon until you reach the desired consistency.

3. Press the piecrust mixture into the bottom and up the sides of a 9-inch pie pan and bake for 10 minutes. Remove and set aside to cool completely.

4. Let the ice cream soften at room temperature for 15 minutes. Spoon the ice cream into the cooled piecrust. Freeze for at least 2 hours.

5. Remove the pie from the freezer, pour the cooled dulce de leche on top, and return to the freezer for at least another hour. Slice into wedges, top with chopped toffee bars, and serve.

Applesauce

SERVES 4-6

PRESSURE TIMING: 2 MINUTES

Applesauce is a sweet snack or, when spooned into a long-stemmed glass and topped with whipped cream, a beautiful dessert. Or leave the whipped cream behind and serve the applesauce with a pork roast.

3 POUNDS APPLES, PEELED, CORED, AND QUARTERED

⅓ CUP APPLE JUICE

1 TABLESPOON FRESH LEMON JUICE

1 TEASPOON GROUND CINNAMON

½ TEASPOON GROUND NUTMEG

1 CUP WHIPPING CREAM

3 TABLESPOONS SUGAR

1. Combine the apples, apple juice, lemon juice, cinnamon, and nutmeg in the pressure cooker; bring the pressure to high (15 psi) and cook for 2 minutes. Use the Quick Release method.

2. Whip the cream with an electric beater until peaks form. Slowly beat in the sugar, one tablespoon at a time. Spoon the applesauce into parfait glasses or bowls and top with whipped cream. Serve immediately.

Stewed Fruit with Mascarpone Cheese

SERVES 4

PRESSURE TIMING: 15 MINUTES

Follow this recipe as-is for an elegant dessert, or leave the sweet, fluffy cheese off of the stewed fruits to make a perfect dish for babies, or anyone who needs soft, nutritious foods.

3 APPLES, PEELED, CORED, AND QUARTERED

3 FIRM PEARS, PEELED, CORED, AND QUARTERED

1 CUP WATER OR FRUIT JUICE OF YOUR CHOICE

2 TABLESPOONS SUGAR

1 TABLESPOON LEMON ZEST

1 CUP MASCARPONE CHEESE

1. Combine the apples, pears, and water in the pressure cooker; bring the pressure to high (15 psi) and cook for 15 minutes. Use the Natural Release method.

2. In the meantime, beat the sugar and lemon zest into the mascarpone cheese.

3. Spoon the stewed fruit into tall stemmed glasses and add a dollop of the sweetened cheese. Serve immediately.

Lemon Custard

Serve this luscious lemon custard with scones or sugar cookies. You'll need four 6-ounce ramekins or glass bowls for this recipe.

2 CUPS MILK

FINELY GRATED ZEST OF 1 LEMON

2 EGGS, LIGHTLY BEATEN

⅓ CUP SUGAR

½ TEASPOON PURE VANILLA EXTRACT

2 CUPS WATER

1. In a large saucepan, heat the milk over medium-high heat and add the lemon zest. Cook, stirring frequently, for 2 minutes. Add the eggs and sugar and cook until the sugar dissolves, about 1 minute. Remove from the heat and stir in the vanilla.

2. Pour the mixture into the ramekins or bowls. Pour the water into the bottom of the pressure cooker. Place the ramekins or bowls on the rack in the cooker. Bring the pressure to high (15 psi) and cook for 20 minutes. Use the Quick Release method. Serve at room temperature or chilled.

Chocolate Pudding with Whipped Cream

SERVES 6

PRESSURE TIMING: 9 MINUTES

This pudding is ready in no time to satisfy your chocolate craving. You'll need four 6-ounce ramekins or glass bowls. Whipped cream is a must.

¼ CUP UNSALTED BUTTER, AT ROOM TEMPERATURE

¾ CUP PLUS 3 TABLESPOONS GRANULATED SUGAR, DIVIDED

¼ CUP BROWN SUGAR, PACKED

2 EGGS

1 EGG YOLK

3 TABLESPOONS UNSWEETENED COCOA

2 TABLESPOONS CORNSTARCH

½ TEASPOON SALT

2 TEASPOONS PURE VANILLA EXTRACT

1¼ CUPS HALF-AND-HALF, AT ROOM TEMPERATURE

½ CUP SEMISWEET MILK OR DARK CHOCOLATE CHIPS

2 CUPS WATER

1 CUP HEAVY CREAM

1. In the bowl of an electric mixer, beat the softened butter, ¾ cup of the granulated sugar, brown sugar, eggs, and additional egg yolk until thoroughly mixed and smooth.

2. In a small bowl, stir together the cocoa, cornstarch, and salt and beat it into the butter mixture. Beat in the vanilla extract. Beat in the half-and-half.

3. Spoon the pudding mixture into the ramekins or glass bowls and top each with chocolate chips. Tent each ramekin with aluminum foil.

continued ▶

4. Pour the water into the bottom of the pressure cooker and place the ramekins on the rack in the cooker. Bring the pressure to high (15 psi) and cook for 9 minutes. Use the Quick Release method.

5. Refrigerate the ramekins for at least 2 hours before serving. When ready to serve, using an electric mixer, beat the heavy cream until peaks begin to form. Add the remaining 3 tablespoons granulated sugar, one tablespoon at a time, and continue beating until the peaks are stiff and the sugar is integrated. Spoon atop the chilled pudding and serve.

Recipe Index

Index

Printed in Great Britain
by Amazon